A Very [illegible]h Revolution

Amirreza Tayebi

Grosvenor House
Publishing Limited

This book is published by
Grosvenor House Publishing Ltd
Link House
140 The Broadway, Tolworth, Surrey, KT6 7HT.
www.grosvenorhousepublishing.co.uk

A CIP record for this book
is available from the British Library

ISBN 978-1-80381-493-3

Dedicated to my beloved father,
the source of inspiration for this book

All the world's a stage,
And all the men and women merely players;
They have their exits and their entrances;
And one man in his time plays many parts.

from As You Like It, by Shakespeare

ABOUT THE AUTHOR

Portrait by Allan Warren

Amirreza Tayebi is a contemporary historian who studied Politics and International Relations at Queen Mary University of London. Before settling in Britain, he attended boarding school in Switzerland and hails from one of Persia's oldest families, the Timurid Dynasty. He currently works in broadcasting and has conducted extensive research on the Swinging Sixties, resulting in the publication of 'A Very British Revolution'. This book explores the themes and influences of that era on modern British culture.

CONTENTS

ACKNOWLEDGEMENTS

I would like to say a very big thank you to all those loyal and lovely people who have been there for me over the years, and to those who encouraged me to write this book, especially my dearest Mummy & Brother. This book would not have been possible without their love and support.

I would also like to extend special thanks to all those legends who agreed to be interviewed for this book among them: Julie Christie, Terence Stamp, Dame Virginia McKenna DBE, James Fox, Susan Hampshire CBE, David Bailey CBE, Amanda Lear, Gered Mankowitz, Lulu, John Swannell, Lady Howard, Peter Noone, Barbara Bouchet, Kenny Jones, Martine Beswick, Nicky Haslam, Amira & Lee Harris, Sir Michael Lindsay-Hogg, Dame Antonia Fraser DBE, Lord Puttnam, Glenda Jackson CBE, Gerald Scarfe CBE, Ray Connolly, Philip Norman, Alvin Rakoff, Gary Raymond, Murray Melvin, Jonathan Aitken, Caroline Munro, Allan Warren, Claudia Cardinale, and the late Terry O'Neill CBE. Finally, I am extremely grateful to my publishing administrator Julie Scott who guided me through the whole production process as well as Clint Hough for kindly providing me a map of the King's Road from the Swinging Sixties which was essential to the completion of this project.

PRELUDE

The 1960s are called the Decade That Never Dies, for its fashions and design come back into vogue again and again and its music seems everlasting. For those, like me, who actually experienced them they were the last thing we expected to follow the boring, colourless 1950s in which we'd spent our childhood. They were in fact a second childhood, with toys and treats we'd never dreamed of and the grown-ups powerless to spoil the party.

Phillip Norman
March 2023

FOREWORD

The ‘Swinging Sixties’ in London was one of the great artistic half-decades in modern artistic history. A group of, mainly, young men found themselves in London. Very like a hundred years earlier, when a group of, mainly, young male painters found themselves in Paris. The Impressionists and the Rock ‘n’ Rollers. Renegades, all of them, scorned because of their art, their looks, their youth, their rebelliousness. At the beginning, both movements were more male-centric, with fewer women of note. But that was to change.

Walking along the King’s Road on a Saturday in 1966 was an experience of pure pleasure. A sunny day, the girls giggling in their short skirts and the guys preening in their new boutique finery, with a Rolling Stones album playing from an open shop door. Young, carefree, in what felt like the Centre of the World at the time.

Sir Michael Lindsay-Hogg April 2023

PREFACE

I have been inspired to write this book mainly by my father who was an active member of the Swinging Sixties, both in London and San Francisco. From an early age, I have developed a fascination for that era which has served me as an escapism in an ever fast-changing world that we live in. I have tended to focus on the intense period of sartorial change ushered in by the Swinging Sixties. It heralded a new era of post-war glamour with the income of young people at its highest since the end of World War II, an increased economic power fuelled a new sense of identity, and an extraordinary creative energy to express it. In the course of writing this book, I have visited all the trendy boutiques, restaurants, and discotheques that were at the helm of 'Swinging London'. I have chronicled the golden era through the experiences, the people and the places that seemed to capture the class unconsciousness spirit of the decade. Furthermore, underlying this, the youth were driven by grit and determination and never compromised the values of loyalty, integrity, and courage that were the legacy of their working class background, nor flinched from challenge whether professional or personal. Finally, this book evokes the splendid vanished worlds that those individuals inhabited while delving into their vivacious, elusive, and imperishable enchantment.

INTRODUCTION

The 1960s were the most exciting times to be alive, partly because the Cultural Revolution, which is often associated with that era, dominated the world at a time of volatility, uncertainty, and ambiguity as tensions were heightening during the Cold War. However, in Britain, things were different in the post-war period. The youth were determined to move on from the destructiveness of the war, which had wrecked their livelihoods and communities in 1950s war-stricken Britain.

In 1963, the Secretary of State for War, John Profumo, was discovered to be having an affair with a woman who was also seeing a Russian military attaché. John Profumo categorically denied the affair but later admitted that he had lied to the House of Commons and resigned. It became known as the Profumo Affair. A scandalous assortment of sex, spies, and government captured the public's attention. The affair changed the relationship between the so-called establishment and the public forever and seriously undermined the public's trust in the establishment. The traditional deference to figures of authority was now gradually being replaced by suspicion and mistrust, as was often portrayed in *Beyond the Fringe* sketches: the first anti-establishment revue performed by Alan Bennett, Dudley Moore, Peter Cook, and Jonathan Miller. Britain began to see the birth of satire in the 1960s, which took aim at the class system and included other shows such as *That Was the Week that Was*, which followed later on.

A gloomy atmosphere had resided within society, and that is partly why the new generation felt it incumbent upon them to shape their own ways of living. Hence, the Swinging Sixties, which for the first time allowed a lot of teenagers from working-class backgrounds to be in control of their lives while maintaining their determination to stop inequalities and injustices that were happening around them. They also manifested their protest through various arts platforms that the youth could relate to.

Meanwhile, fashion in the sixties mirrored many of the social changes of the decade. Mary Quant became famous for popularising the miniskirt and hotpants, which defined the fashions of that era in Britain. The mini was designed to be free and liberating for women. Her fashion sense of designs using simple geometric shapes and colours gave women a new kind of femininity. Women were free to wear more playful, youthful clothes that would have been regarded as immoral the decade before.

As for music, by the early 1960s, the British had developed a viable national music industry and began to produce adapted forms of American rock 'n' roll in beat music and British blues. These would be quintessential to the so-called British Invasion, which re-exported to America via bands such as the Beatles, the Shadows, the Animals, Small Faces, the Kinks, the Yardbirds and the Rolling Stones.

And lastly, for the film industry, the determined, northern working-class focus that had already transformed British theatre at the beginning of the decade prevailed, with films such as *Saturday Night and Sunday Morning* (1960), *A Taste of Honey* (1963) and *This Sporting Life* (1963), respectively directed by Karel Weisz, Tony Richardson, and Lindsey Anderson.

By 1964, the focus was back on London, mainly thanks to the popularity of the Beatles, who developed a more complex screen presence in a hugely successful film called *A Hard Day's Night*, which added confidence to the already thriving music and fashion scene that was envied worldwide. Albeit, the Swinging London films seemed to be increasingly focused on revealing the failure of their protagonists to get in on the boom – *The Knack ...and How To Get It* (1965), *Georgy Girl* (1966), and *Poor Cow* (1967) – and the emptiness of the scene was exposed in highly controversial *Darling* (1965).

Notwithstanding, the Swinging city drew several foreign directors to London to make some memorable films of the decade. Michelangelo Antonioni with *Blow-Up* (1966) delivered an unusually acute 'Swinging London' movie, while Roman Polanski brought his somewhat bleak vision to *Repulsion* (1965). In addition, there were the French nouvelle vague pioneers such as

François Truffaut (*Fahrenheit 451*) and Jean-Luc Godard (*Sympathy for the Devil*).

The 1960s was a decade of rapid change that allowed people to win back the liberty, freedom and individuality they had fought for from the shackles of the so-called establishment. Those people who brought about change within society were full of confidence, hope and optimism for a better future, prompting them to embark on a journey transcending generations, which still fascinates, intrigues and stimulates conversations with regard to that extraordinary era. And here is the story of how that journey began.

I. TIMES THEY ARE A-CHANGING

In the early 1960s, the world was undergoing extraordinary socio-economic upheavals triggered by post-war prosperity. Adolescent defiance, empowerment, and confidence were becoming the social fabric of society while socio-religious rules were crumbling. The so-called new establishment was working-class young boys and girls consisting of a 'swinging meritocracy' of actors, photographers, pop stars, and writers. The tectonic social and cultural shifts across Britain as the nation emerged from post-war fatigue chronicled how youth hijacked fashion, the arts, music, and film to herald a new era which later on was universally acclaimed as the Swinging Sixties.

They were mostly from humble backgrounds and sported their distinct regional accents like badges. They previously felt ignored by the establishment and now thrived on having their voice heard and listened to, on the adrenalin of delivering creativity as their driving force and fearlessly rejecting the snobby conservatism of the 1950s. Before 1963, youth largely felt subservient in the society they were living in. But that was soon to fade away with the so-called new social aristocracy and inspired new standards for society as a whole to adopt.

In the spring of 1963, the legendary film director, Joseph Losey, who had been living in London since leaving America because of his past association with communism and being expelled by McCarthy, was now observing a social and cultural shift in London society, particularly with youth on a mission to break down existing conventions to create and innovate a new freewheeling era. While observing the society, Joseph Losey came up with the idea of a film which was an attack on the British class system, which showed the first ever glimpses into the Swinging Sixties era, called *The Servant*. It was the first film in Britain to have addressed issues such as power, pleasure, sexuality, and the breakdown of the class system all at once in one film.

The project seemed to be coming together when RADA graduates, Sarah Miles and James Fox, were asked to the first night of Jimmy Woolf's production of Bryan Forbes' film *The L-Shaped Room*. At the premiere party, they were placed on a table with Dirk Bogarde's lifelong partner and manager, Tony Forwood. On behalf of Dirk Bogarde, he suggested a role for them in a new film called *The Servant*. He invited them to go and see them at the Connaught the next day for a drink before lunch. The conversation quickly got back to how wonderful *The L-Shaped Room* had been, but their minds were on what had just happened: encountering the great Dirk Bogarde and being offered to work alongside him in his next film.

For these young actors, this was surely a night to remember. They got up early the following day and made ready to meet Dirk Bogarde for drinks before lunch. After they arrived in the lounge of the Connaught Hotel, they were ushered by the staff to Dirk Bogarde's suite where they were greeted in the corridor on the third floor by the great man himself. He was wearing an elegant grey suit with casual black moccasins from Gucci, with a Guinness and a Kent cigarette on the go.

James Fox and Sarah Miles relaxed in the comfortable armchairs until they were joined by the somewhat sullen film director, Joseph Losey, who was going to direct *The Servant*. The reason he was grumpy on that particular day was because one of his films had been massacred in an unauthorised version and he intended to sue the company. But shortly after, both James Fox and Sarah Miles were given a script for *The Servant* by his secretary. Shortly before they left, while showing them to the door, Dirk Bogarde told James Fox why he had decided to cast him in his next film, which was because he had tremendously enjoyed watching *The Door* on television, a play with Ann Todd.

The storyline was unusual and arresting. Tony, a wealthy young aristocrat, sets himself up in a Chelsea house and needs someone to run it for him. He is engaged to Susan (Wendy Craig) and dabbles in business. Barrett applies for the job and impresses Tony with his ideas. ("Simple and classical is best, I always think, sir.") He gets the job – plans the menus, runs the bar, arranges the flowers and upsets the fiancée. Tony is rather protective. "I think we need a girl, sir, to help in the house."

To which Tony enquires, "Girl, what sort of girl?"

"A maid," Barrett responds.

"Oh, do you?" asks Tony.

"Yes, sir, they can be very useful," adds Barrett. This is the first time the audience senses that Barrett is acting as some sort of pimp, arranging his sister for the master.

Vera is introduced as Barrett's sister. Unsisterly goings-on occur in the top-floor bedroom. One night Vera offers herself to Tony, hoisting herself up on the kitchen table. Tony is hooked on Vera. But coming back early one weekend, Tony and Susan find Barrett and Vera together in Tony's bed. He throws them both out of the house.

However, Tony can't manage on his own. Barrett returns to say sorry, and Tony has him back. Barrett gets Vera back and plays hide-and-seek and ball games on the stairs with Tony. Barrett invites other friends to the house and then introduces Tony to a potion from a gentleman in Jermyn Street. Tony becomes zombie-like. Barrett promises to mend his ways but is now more dominant than Tony. The end! Harold Pinter had created a riveting drama.

James Fox's father had now read it, and though he had reservations about his ability to do it, he thought it was very effective and contained a good part for Sarah. But he still wanted to do a screen test for his son, paid out of his own pocket. He wanted to see whether or not his son could manage the last scenes where his character, Tony, is on drugs. Therefore he hired a studio and crew and set him up with half a tumbler of brandy, let it work, and asked his son to say some of the lines to him, standing by the camera. He topped up his glass every now and then and, apparently satisfied, got him back to his flat to sober up.

The next thing, having found their Tony, Joseph Losey and Norman Priggen, the producers of the film, wanted was to find the money, which they eventually did. Next, Joseph Losey had a wonderful idea to help his leading actor, James Fox, as Tony, with his approach to filming. He proposed that he work for two weeks prior to shooting with an actor/director he knew called Vivian Matalon.

As a result of that suggestion, James Fox went to Viv's flat in West London rather nervously. He seemed to admire the script and was extremely interested in it. He wanted to be coached so he would be prepared and confident before they got to the camera. Vivian introduced him to a rewarding system of approaching a part.

Even though the character James Fox was playing, Tony, was close to his own experience and temperament, he still needed to understand how to communicate that. They worked on some intentions for each scene. Some were easier than others, but in Harold Pinter's dialogue, there is room for the sub-text and interior dialogue to be developed. It was important for the actors, as much as it was for the rest of the crew, to discover these layers, which were critical to the understanding of the film.

The interview with Barrett was the first and hardest scene. It was virtually a monologue for him. Here it was essential that James Fox could move and say the lines comfortably, telling Barrett what his job entailed. They explored his attitude towards the other characters. Tony really thinks of Barrett as a fussy old maid, but he feels that one has to put up with one's servants. Notwithstanding, Tony's feelings for Susan are mixed. He likes her physically but wants her to like Barrett too. Vera awakens unexpressed desires and exposes chinks in Tony's suavity.

Little does he know that Barrett is, in fact, pulling the strings by effecting the seduction in the hope that he can use this as leverage over the master – implying and hinting at his own homosexuality but covertly as it was glossed over in the screenplay by Harold Pinter. This was unlike the book by Robert Maugham, where there were explicit references drawing on his own homosexual experiences. In 1963, homosexuality in Britain was still a criminal act and, therefore, still a taboo for filmmakers and screenwriters to explicitly refer to it in films.

Another scene the actors found hard was the ball game on the stairs. They decided that the solution was to play it as if Tony really wanted to win and enjoyed poking fun at Barrett's poor gamesmanship. The hide-and-seek scene evolved through discussing it and trying different approaches. Many people have found this one of the most effective scenes in the film.

However, all the essence of the film culminates in the final dance of the psychological death scene, where Tony feels ashamed once he finally realises he has succumbed to Barrett's manipulation of him. This was replete with the sexual seduction strategy influenced by Vera, herself oblivious that she's been used as a proxy by her own brother, Barrett, as part of his revenge against aristocracy and the hierarchy inherent in London society: the so-called enemy within. However, Barrett is also left with a feeling of shame for having been trifled with by his master, leaving no clear victor in that dangerous game that he played out.

For the drug scenes at the end, Joseph Losey had some ghastly glycerine drops put in James Fox's eyes to make them blurred and watery. He also decided that James Fox needed to bleach his hair, and 'Bumble' Dawson supplied some nice clothes. They shot nearly all of it in Shepperton Studios within ten weeks, even though Joseph Losey had to be off the film for a week with pneumonia. His direction was meticulous, knowing every single aspect, detail and element that had to be underlined in the film. *The Servant* is a careful dissection of class and sex in sixties society, with Joseph Losey implying implicitly that the working-class are taking over from the aristocracy.

But the actors in the film, including James Fox, only appreciated it fully when they saw what he had created on the screen. It was hard to recognise anything of Dirk Bogarde's natural self in the malevolent character he was playing. They became good friends and sat drinking coffee and chatting for hours in his caravan on the set.

Conspicuously, throughout the shooting, both leading actors in *The Servant* – James Fox and Dirk Bogarde – had a close working relationship, but their friendship went even beyond that. James Fox became a regular visitor on Sundays to his house near Guildford. Both actors shared many things in common – his home, walking with the dogs, talking about the business and the garden and country life, about which Dirk Bogarde was very knowledgeable. In the sixties, before Dirk Bogarde left to live in France, he had an attractive circle of friends such as John and Jill Standing, and Noel and Sarah Harrison.

At the same time, both actors never talked directly about their roles or what they were doing in the film. They just let what had been soaked into them about their parts come out on the set. Joseph Losey's direction and the script made it work.

On the last day of the film, James Fox and his entourage were in a pub in Chelsea when suddenly he got in an awful panic when he thought he would never act again, feeling with a cold shock that he had lost all of his talent. The next day he rang Dirk Bogarde, who was by that point used to end-of-picture let-downs and told him how hard it was for him, too, to take off his character's clothes from the film and put them back in the trunk. Conversely, they both endured a difficult time while waiting for the film to be released.

Finally, when the film was to open, James Fox invited Jackie Lane to attend the premiere while Sarah Miles, his on-off partner since their RADA days, invited

Swinging Sixties heartthrob Terence Stamp. The cracks were beginning to grow larger in the relationship. But, as far as they were concerned, all they could think of that night and the following day was the brilliant reception it was given by the crew at the flat on Royal Avenue, located just off the King's Road where the film's exterior scenes were shot.

II. A HARD DAY'S NIGHT

At the beginning of 1964, technological advancements drastically changed how people spent their leisure time. The increase in employment in factories and the increase in money allowed people to spend more on leisure activities. Black and white television and pocket transistor radios allowed people to spend their free time listening to music and watching TV. *Juke Box Jury* (BBC), *Top of the Pops* (BBC), and *Ready Steady Go* (ITV), presented by David Jacobs for the BBC, and Cathy McGown for ITV, occupied the schedule of young teenagers day after day as they watched their favourite pop bands singers and idols on those programmes. The film director, Dick Lester, decided to make his next film based on the sheer enthusiasm of the young teenagers at the time by making a film based on the magnificent screenplay written by Alun Owen: *A Hard Day's Night*. The film portrays 36 hours of frenzy in the life of the Beatles as they prepare for a television performance.

Notwithstanding, the King's Road had also become like an exclusive school playground. Everyone went to the same parties, the same shops, the same coffee bars, bistros and pubs. And on Saturdays, if you weren't parading up and down the King's Road, actors, musicians, and artists hung out at clubs like the Arethusa and restaurants such as the Picasso and the Casserole, all on the King's Road. Furthermore, there was also Mr Chow's restaurant in Knightsbridge; he was going out at the time with the fashion model and one of the faces of the Swinging Sixties, Grace Coddington. Still on the King's Road were quirky little boutiques, like Granny Takes a Trip, owned by Nigel Weymouth, who was a painter, and John Pearce. They sold paintings, posters and clothes – crushed velvet trousers and fitted jackets with thin arms in wonderful greens and burgundies.

However, the most prestigious boutiques on the King's Road belonged to Mary Quant, one of the first designers to have a boutique there. It was called Bazaar and, with her husband, Alexander Plunkett Greene, she went on to build up a chain, then brought out a range of make-up and was very influential in how people looked and dressed. There were models such as Jean Shrimpton, Marianne Faithfull, Anita Pallenberg and Pattie Boyd, who were regular customers at Bazaar around the winter of 1963.

The latter, who had previously signed up to a model agency and who had already posed for magazines such as *Vogue*, was becoming a successful fashion model. In December that year, she had moved in with fellow model Mary Bee at a tiny flat on Oakley Street, Chelsea, cohabiting in the same bedroom together. The following month, in January 1964, Pattie Boyd was busy working with a photographer called Dudley

Harris one morning when her agent, Cherry Marshall, rang to tell her she had made an appointment for her at a casting session. It would take place at one o'clock in the Hilton Hotel, Park Lane, and the contact was Walter Shenson.

At first, she assumed it was an advertising agency job, given she was used to those interviews. When she got there, to her surprise, was the director Dick Lester, who had previously directed her in a few tv commercials a year earlier for Smith's crisps, leading the casting auditions. She asked Dick Lester if it was yet another advertising job, but he wouldn't give it away. Soon it became apparent, thanks to her agent, Cheryl, what the project would be. It was top secret, but Dick Lester had just offered her the opportunity to play a part in his upcoming Beatles film, *A Hard Day's Night*.

After hearing the news that she had been signed up to the Beatles' upcoming film, she began feeling apprehensive and sought to withdraw her application. She thought at the time she had never aspired to become an actress, and the idea of having to act in front of a camera terrified her. However, due to her agent's insistence, she accepted the role of a schoolgirl dressed in uniform for two days' work. Although she had a job to get on with, she felt rather embarrassed wearing a school uniform on set throughout the filming.

At that time, Britain was in the early stages of Beatlemania, a few years after performing at nightclubs in Hamburg and at the Cavern in Liverpool. In less than a year, they had gone from being a talented group with a strong following in the north to major recording artists with millions of fans worldwide, fame, acclaim, and the stardom that every rock star dreams of. The four lads with their Vidal Sassoon haircuts – John Lennon, Paul McCartney, George Harrison, and Ringo Starr – had already conquered Europe, and before they started shooting this film, they took America by a storm – a notoriously difficult task for British musicians, making them the first British band to ever have global success.

In the early 1960s, they had not yet made it in the United States. But thanks to their success in Europe, where they first started by honing their skills and building their reputation playing at nightclubs in Liverpool and Hamburg, and inspiring Beatlemania that had captured the continent, their manager, Brian Epstein, sensed that it was forthcoming. Their success in America was not a matter of 'if', but 'when'.

It was only the following year that the Beatles caused the British Invasion in other continents too with their first big hit, 'I want to hold your hand', which went straight to number one. And in February 1964, they staged the British Invasion of America by appearing on *The Ed Sullivan Show* in New York, one of the most popular chat shows in the United States at the time. With an estimated audience of 90 million plus, it was the most watched show in America in 1964 – a record that was not beaten by any band or single artists for some time to come, establishing the Beatles' international fame.

By early 1964, the Beatles' songs and albums had already reached number one in every best-seller UK chart. *Please Please Me* was the top-selling LP, 'Twist and Shout' was the number one and 'She loves You' had already outsold every other single. This allowed them to shape popular culture for an entire generation, push the boundaries of contemporary music, and become one of the most iconic, influential and best-selling British music artists of all time.

The instructions for Pattie Boyd's first day's filming on *A Hard Day's Night* were to go to Paddington Station and meet three other models, who had also been cast a schoolgirls, under the clock in the morning, then join a train halfway down platform one. But to their surprise and much to their curiosity, no more information was actually communicated to them.

About 10 minutes out of London, it ground to an unexpected halt at a tiny station, deserted but for four familiar faces, who leapt on board and bounced into their compartment to greet them. They introduced themselves fleetingly, John Lennon made a crack and the models all laughed, then they bounced out. The fab four were enchanting, and the models cursed their luck to be meeting them in gymslips.

The film crew had taken over the train, and most of the action happened on the move. It was supposedly about two days in the life of the Beatles, and the train scene began with the four racing into a station, chased by hundreds of screaming fans, then jumping into a train that pulled away, leaving the fans forlornly on the platform. They had done that bit at Marylebone Station before they met up with the models. They were involved in the action once they had supposedly jumped into the carriage.

The train took the models to Cornwall and back; they spent most of the day watching the action, chatting to everyone during the breaks and waiting to do their scene. Throughout the filming, the Beatles were so funny together, so quick-witted, and their laughter seemed infectious. However, none of the models could understand half of what they said because of the thick Liverpudlian accent – a revelation to them, given they had never heard anything like it at that point. They also found it impossible to be in their company and not be helpless with laughter.

On first impressions, John seemed more cynical and brash than the others. Ringo, the most endearing, Paul was cute, and George, with velvet-brown eyes and dark chestnut hair, was the best-looking man Pattie Boyd had ever seen. At lunch, she found herself sitting next to him; whether by accident or design, she has never been sure.

Although they shared a lot of characteristics in common, both being shy, and spoke barely a word to one other, they unequivocally found each other's company absolutely electrifying. As the train neared London and the filming was winding down, Pattie Boyd felt sad that such a magical time was ending. It had been pure joy, and she just wanted to capture it forever. Abruptly, at the end of the train scene filming, George Harrison dashed to see Pattie Boyd, who was about to be transported back to London.

He saw her in the models' compartment packing, approached her and asked her to marry him, at which she laughed, assuming it was merely a Beatles' joke as she had to all Beatles jokes previously. She scarcely allowed herself to wonder why he had said it or whether he might feel as she did as well.

She felt awkward at George Harrison's proposal to her after merely a few days past their first encounter and was not sure whether he was being serious or just playing. Therefore she played it safe by telling him that although she had a boyfriend at the time, she didn't mind George hanging out with them, which subsequently resulted in them marrying a year and a half after their encounter on that train.

Apart from that fairytale triggered on the film's set, *A Hard Day's Night* captures the unconventional spirit of a country teetering on the brink of a cultural revolution. Although the film is in black and white, it's the epitome of the colourful cultural revolution that a post-war starved Britain was undergoing, with the Beatles being the epicentre of that crest of the wave in the 1960s. In other words, it also documents the emergence from a rationing-dependent nation towards economic and social prosperity with natural charm, an eye for detail and absurdist humour.

Notwithstanding, it was also a much-cherished experience for the director of the film, Richard Lester. He developed a sort of affinity with John Lennon, who he admired enormously, casting him in yet another film of his: *How I Won The War* (1967). He valued Ringo Starr, the actor around whom Alun

Owen's script made the story evolve, for his natural instinct and persona, which resulted in a great rapport with the camera. Paul McCartney was a bit over-enthusiastic, trying harder than he should have throughout the film. He profusely enjoyed directing George Harrison, who he believed, was the easiest and most effective Beatle to work with, and always took Dick Lester's directions assiduously.

Despite the seeming spontaneity of *A Hard Day's Night*, only three scenes —John Lennon's scene where he's lying in the bath, the station scene when they get out of the train and get into a cab chased by thousands of their supporters, which takes up a minute or two in the film, and lastly the press conference where the actors posed as journalists – were unscripted. The questions were in the script, but the Beatles did not know them in advance, and they were about to find out at the same time as the audience, which adds to the realism of the film, as well as its natural lighting and tight cutting.

The songs credited in the film and also released as a soundtrack album were composed by Paul McCartney and John Lennon for the film, and the instrumentals were recorded by the George Martin Orchestra at Abbey Road Studios. They include, 'A Hard Day's Night' (opening credits), 'I Should Have Known Better', 'I Wanna Be Your Man', 'Don't Bother Me', 'All My Loving', 'If I Fell', 'Can't Buy Me Love', 'And I Love Her', 'I'm Happy Just to Dance with You', 'This Boy', 'Can't Buy Me Love', 'Tell Me Why', and 'She Loves You'.

The film was a phenomenal success, with critics calling it one of the smoothest, freshest and funniest films ever made. In the UK, it was the second highest grossing film in 1964 with £11 million against the £189,000 it cost Walter Shenson Films to produce, finishing second behind Stanley Kubrick's *Dr Strangelove* that year.

After the phenomenal success of *A Hard Day's Night*, the director, Richard Lester, was approached to make yet another emblematic film of the Swinging Sixties London cultural phenomenon: *The Knack ... and How to Get It*. To convey the story, which was based on a play of the same name by Ann Jellicoe, he had to borrow from the French New Wave in terms of his visual trickery, with oddly-edited sequences resulting in unexpected jump cuts, humorous subtitles, and freeze-frames throughout the film. Jean-Luc Godard was the main influence, given the two had also met in the same year.

Both films had a lot in common, depicting the sexual revolution, which was rampant during the Swinging London Sixties. A young schoolmaster, Colin (Michael Crawford), working in London, without any past sexual experience, wishes to gain the 'knack' of flirtation. Thanks to his neighbour Tolen's (Ray Brooks) knowledge of seduction skills, he indulges in a relationship with an inexperienced, shy and innocent Nancy Jones (Rita Tushingham). Nancy is a young woman who has arrived in London from the suburbs to work for the Young Women's Christian Association. It ends as they begin a new life by moving in together.

Dick Lester remains one of the few directors who captured the spirit of the 1960s – a period of rapid social and cultural change, with youth urging the establishment to have their voices heard while pushing for change in that direction. As a director, in both films, *A Hard Day's Night* and *The Knack ...and How to Get it*, he places London at the centre of that transformation from the bleak, conservative city, only just beginning to forget the troubles of the Second World War, into the capital of the world, full of freedom, hope, and promise. It was the centre of all excitement, the city where anything and everything seemed possible.

The trio of principal actors, Michael Crawford (Colin), Rita Tushingham (Nancy Jones), and Ray Brooks (Tolen), all add to that excitement by giving bravura performances. The locations, featuring some rather dingy-looking parts of the capital, look all the more so thanks to the decision to film in monochrome. This was particularly brave considering the colourful times the film was depicting. The one ingredient that most of all created the sense of playfulness indicative of the film was John Barry's wonderfully mischievous jazz-tinged pop score.

Jane Birkin, Charlotte Rampling, and Jacqueline Bisset, who were originally models at the beginning of their careers, all made their first cinematic appearances in the film. Moreover, the director of the film, Dick Lester, also made a cameo in the film, making it the only time he has appeared in his own films. He is seen in one of the reaction shots in probably one of the most famous scenes when Nancy, Colin and Tom roll the bed through the streets after finding it at a scrapyard where Colin and Tom had just met Nancy. Dick Lester was the guy standing next to another helping them with the bed, having got the inspiration from Alfred Hitchcock, who often made cameos in his films.

The film was yet another phenomenal success for Dick Lester, who had experienced the same success with *A Hard Day's Night* the year before. But this time, *The Knack ...and How to Get It* won that year's Palme d'Or at the Cannes Film Festival, making it the first ever Swinging Sixties London film to have earned such an international accolade.

The critics called it a delightful film that was beautifully shot and praised Rita Tushingham's performance as 'ground-breaking'. It made a net profit of £1.5 million, more than compensating the film's budget, which was £165,000. It was produced by Windfall productions, which was established in the late 1950s by Tony Richardson, John Osborne, and Harry Saltzman.

III. MY GENERATION

During the Swinging Sixties, filmgoers started to see London through the eyes of foreign filmmakers, among them Jean-Luc Godard, François Truffaut, Michelangelo Antonioni, and Roman Polanski. They captured undercurrents of paranoia, madness, and violence that seemed inherent within society but were still taboo at that point to show on the big screens, but they were among the first directors to have reflected it.

One of those giants of the sixties, Roman Polanski, often liked to drive around Chelsea in a sports car with bimbos clustering on the upholstery like bats and to roister the small hours away in nightclubs blue with funk and reefers.

A lot of people admired his courage and his talent but he reccived mixed reviews when it came to his style. John Fraser was on holiday in the South of France when he was offered the leading role opposite Catherine Deneuve in Roman Polanski's first English-speaking picture set in the Swinging Sixties, called *Repulsion*. He was playing Colin, an edgy and odd character with some unresolved anger or violence, and despite making several attempts to woo the female character, she seemed uninterested in him.

John Fraser had been impressed with *Knife in the Water*, which was one of Roman Polanski's early films as a director, so he accepted the role in the film without seeing the script. However, when he read it on his return from the South of France to England, he found the script somewhat disturbing and uncomfortable to act in a few scenes. In the studio, he had to embark upon an onslaught of scenes in which he had to act dead, fully clothed, and with his eyes underwater.

He was taken by surprise when he realised how emotionally demanding his character was meant to be, but given he had already signed a contract for the film, he was bound to stay with the crew to the end of the filming.

Although he found it disconcerting in terms of staying in character while filming in the thick of the traffic in South Kensington, where passersby were in the way of him and Catherine Deneuve asking for their autographs. Despite this, both actors deemed working with Roman Polanski as the best director for actors they have ever worked with.

The screenplay was written by a French writer, Gerard Brach, who was approached by Roman Polanski to do a very strong and grabbing kind of film. Their wish at the outset was to make a film that frightened people and was centred on fear. And gradually they wrote it in three weeks – no more. Roman Polanski, at the time, knew of a girl living in Saint Germain, at the centre of Paris, who, despite having stunning features – young, delicate, and sweet – also had a violent clash between her look and inner being, which inspired Roman Polanski into adapting it for his next feature film. As a result, *Repulsion* is a fairly intense film about female psychology.

The film is scary, suspenseful, and full of an atmosphere of foreboding. Before the filming started, there was a kind of split between the writers, Roman Polanski and Gerard Brach, with the producers on their respective ideas. The producers thought they were going to make something very trivial, but the writers were thinking, *How can you change your own nature?* So they made *Repulsion* which gradually edges towards being a serious film on schizophrenia – a particular case study. Added to the script was the superb photography by Gil Taylor, using very wide angles to get the emotional warping and mania of the main protagonist, played by Catherine Deneuve.

Repulsion depicts the story of a manicurist in the middle of Swinging Sixties London, and is set in Chelsea. Carol, portrayed by Catherine Deneuve, is left alone in her sister's flat in South Kensington and has a mental breakdown, hallucinating lecherous, leering British men on the street, in the pub, and forcing themselves on her at home. Despite looking like a sexual dream, she had feelings of a nightmare over her body, exhibiting the early stages of schizophrenia.

The remaining cast included Ian Hendry as Michael, her sister's lover, Patrick Wymark as the landlord, and Yvonne Furneaux as her sister, Helen.

Although *Repulsion* got an X certificate upon its release in Britain, it was a huge success both with the critics and at the box office, with a margin profit of £3 million despite costing only £75,000 for its distributors to make. It enjoyed a worldwide success and won the Golden Bear for best film at the Berlin Film Festival.

After the release of *Repulsion* on 10 June 1965, Catherine Deneuve became a revered French icon in Britain during the sixties. At the end of filming *Repulsion,* Catherine Deneuve met the sixties photographer David Bailey at the Ad Lib Club, which was, by 1965, the big disco in London situated in a penthouse just behind the Empire Cinema, Leicester Square.

It was owned by a nightclub impresario called Bran Morris. What made the club so great was the fact that one found oneself alongside the people who had made the music. The Beatles and the Stones would be grooving around on the dance floor. In the dark corners you could occasionally see Terence Stamp romancing Julie Christie or David Bailey wooing Catherine Deneuve, and in another corner would be Roman Polanski with Sharon Tate, and everybody who was anybody was there, and so was everybody who was nobody but going to be somebody tomorrow.

There was the buzz every night of dreams coming true and the charge of fresh dreams that may come true sometime soon. And the shock as a record was played for the first time ever, and you knew you were listening to a pop classic being born, and the new young genius who wrote it said 'sorry' as he stepped on your toe as they all whirled like dervishes round the dance floor and into the history of their own chosen field of endeavour.

Polanski wanted Bailey to photograph Catherine Deneuve for *Playboy* to promote *Repulsion*. But Deneuve didn't want to be photographed for *Playboy*, and Bailey disliked the idea of it. However, much to Polanski's persistence and charm, and on the condition she could pick the pictures, she agreed to it.

Shortly after their encounter to shoot her for *Playboy* magazine, Bailey and Deneuve tied the knot at St. Pancras Town Hall in the summer of 1965. The ceremony joined together, as some the papers called it at the time, the reigning monarchs of the in-crowd of the Swinging Sixties. During the heat of 1965, a trendy, influential '60s storyline called *Darling* – in flashy form and cynical content – caught the eyes of John Schlesinger and Frederic Raphael.

John Schlesinger and Frederic Raphael built *Darling* around Julie Christie as Diana Scott, an attractive and ambitious young woman determined to lead her own life. The film unequivocally depicts an original conception of a changing society, somewhat pretentious and hypocritical, never shown before on big screens.

As the 'darling' of the title, Christie was Diana Scott, an unscrupulously ambitious model whose empty character mirrored the tinsel world of sixties chic. Determined to advance her career at any cost, she manipulates a series of men, falling in love with one (Bogarde) by whom she becomes pregnant. She aborts the baby, reasoning that it interferes with her work, takes up with the mean and equally manipulative Miles Brand (Laurence Harvey) and loses Dirk Bogarde's character when she gets drawn into a life of sexual high jinks. After decadent adventures, she opts for retirement and marriage with Prince Cesare della Romita (José Louis de Vilallonga), residing with him in strained splendour at his palace in Florence. Finally, seeing the wastefulness of her life, she strips off the uniform of wealth, quits Italy and flies back to Bogarde to attempt, unsuccessfully, a fresh start.

However, there was a dilemma to choreograph for both Freddy Raphael and John Schlesinger during the last scene. Julie Christie's character strips off her clothes as she saunters through the vacant, chilly palace. It is to demonstrate that despite having wealth, everything, she still decided to strip naked to symbolise the lonely, naked creature underneath. A profound moment, central to the theme: an unambiguous depiction of naked, imperfect reality that contrasts the fairy tale of Diana's life: a showcase of derision for traditional conformity.

For a start, Julie Christie refused to strip for cameras, beginning to detest the character of Diana, and, besides, she thought her nude body unattractive; at some point she was going to quit. But in the end, much to John Schlesinger's relief, she changed her mind and decided to do it. After the release, Diana Scott became a Swinging Sixties icon, a symbol of rebellion and success, rebellion and decline, with teenagers adopting the sexy, mini-skirted Diana as their standard-bearer. The success of *Darling* was to be the start of a virtual cult of Julie Christie and elevated her to a place in sixties fashionable icons. She had become the cinematic face of the 1960s and, as such, the embodiment of what was now being called Swinging London.

Darling was both a critical and commercial success, grossing £9 million at the worldwide box office against a budget of only £350,000. It was nominated for three Academy Awards, winning two of them, including earning an academy award for Julie Christie the following year, making her the youngest British actress ever to have won it.

IV. WHAT'S ALL ABOUT TOWN

In spring of 1965, a hairstylist from south London created one of the most iconic hairstyles of the time. He was responsible for the close-cut and geometric hairstyle called the bob cut, also known as the 'Nancy Kwan cut', creating the most iconic looks of that era for Mary Quant and Nancy Kwan. It was in one of Vidal Sassoon's salons in London that the idea of adapting a stage play into a film with the character becoming the epitome of cool in Swinging Sixties London.

One Friday morning in the heat of summer in June 1966, Hylda Gilbert, the wife of film director Lewis Gilbert, was at one of Vidal Sassoon's salons in London when she found herself sitting next to actress Margaret Courtney. She was full of a new play she had just opened in. It was doing very well, and she was sure it would make a good film. Hylda, not one to hang around, took a friend and went to the Mermaid where it was playing. She went home very excited and asked her husband, Lewis Gilbert, to urgently go and see it, given it really would make a good film, which he did right away. *Alfie,* the story of a handsome cockney who gets what he wants – women, mostly – while absolutely making no commitments to them, was set in the Swinging Sixties in London. John Neville, a leading actor of the same generation as Richard Burton, was playing the part of Alfie.

The subject fascinated Lewis Gilbert because he believed Alfie was a new kind of hero; although far from admirable, he had a cockiness and an energy that was injected into the real life of 1960s London. Good-looking men, born into the working classes, were making names for themselves as photographers, tailors, hairdressers, and leading actors, which had not happened previously. Therefore, Lewis Gilbert knew instinctively he was going to get the rights to the play.

The author was Bill Naughton, and his name was surprisingly familiar. He had contributed short stories to *Men Only*, a monthly magazine which had been very popular with servicemen during the Blitz.

Therefore, he decided to contact Bernard Miles, who ran the Mermaid theatre and duly put him in touch with the author, Bill Naughton. He said, to Lewis Gilbert's great joy, that no one had applied for the rights before, and he would be delighted to give him the rights to make a film version of *Alfie*. Bill Naughton then wrote his screenplay and brought it to him. However, Lewis Gilbert took issue with the second act when Alfie contracts tuberculosis and spends virtually the whole of the act in hospital. As a result, Lewis Gilbert took the initiative of breaking the scenes up and seeking visual ways of showing what previously had been spoken. In any case, had they left the hospital act in, the film would have been longer. Bill Naughton was not particularly amused by that decision, but nor did he try to obstruct the film crew.

And now came the problem of raising money, which was beginning to take its toll. It was soon resolved when Lewis Gilbert, one day out in Shaftsbury Avenue, bumped into his long-term film mogul friend, Leslie Grade, who suggested Lewis Gilbert go to the office the next day and discuss the film budget with him and his brother, Bernie. But, by the time the script of *Alfie* was finished, the Woolf brothers were also showing an interest in joining the Grades on the project, implying the finance issue was no longer an obstacle to setting a date for shooting the film, which was mostly set in London.

It was time to get down to some work that was a bit more creative – casting. Who was going to play this new kind of hero in this kind of world where the advent of the contraceptive pill meant that young men and women were free to make love to whom they liked when they liked, and most definitely did? Jimmy Woolf wanted his protégé, Laurence Harvey, to play the part to Lewis Gilbert's dismay. He had previous experience of directing Laurence Harvey in his three early films in the 1950s but believed that audience's ears were becoming gradually more attuned to the different accents you can find in Britain. He therefore adamantly sought to cast an effortless cockney in *Alfie*.

Lewis Gilbert also sensed that the Woolf brothers were now less interested in financing the film, given their first choice of actor Laurence Harvey in the lead part had been rejected.

The following month, Lewis Gilbert was set to travel to America to meet two new heads taking over Paramount, who turned out to be both writers as well. Subsequently, after having read the script, they decided they would finance the whole film. Therefore, Lewis Gilbert was given a contract to the effect that Paramount would be doing the financing but would not question the casting. The film cost Paramount £250,000.

When Lewis Gilbert was still in Hollywood, he set up a meeting with Terence Stamp, who was also in Hollywood filming *The Collector* with William Wyler. He desperately wanted to play the part for nothing. Lewis Gilbert, acting cautiously, offered Terence Stamp the part on Broadway first. But he was unaware of his inexperience of acting on stage. He thought it was courageous of Terence Stamp to give it a go on stage, but Paramount decided perhaps it would be to the benefit of everyone involved with the film that a more experienced stage actor played the part.

The word got around thanks to Lewis Gilbert's son, John – who as a young man was very much a product of the Swinging London in terms of music, fashion, and actors – that Terence Stamp had a flatmate while living on Ebury Street behind Sloane Square in Chelsea. This flatmate was also a cockney actor and very good-looking too. He was called Michael Caine, and he would make the perfect Alfie.

The main driving force of Alfie in the film is merely to seduce women during the Swinging Sixties. For the women in the story, Bill Naughton wrote a series of female characters, including Ruby, Alfie's equal for tactics, played by Shelley Winters, who was very feminine in the part as well as tough.

Another part was played by Jane Asher, who plays a northern, country girl who keeps Alfie happy with her cooking. There was a bedroom scene halfway through the film with Michael Caine in which she appeared to be clad in one of Alfie's shirts and nothing else. As this shirt was not transparent and was about the same length as the miniskirts that were all the rage at the time, they thought that modesty was being upheld, and there was nothing inappropriate or salacious about the scene.

However, around this time, Jane Asher's boyfriend was none other than Paul McCartney. The director, Lewis Gilbert, was discreetly informed by a messenger on the set that McCartney did not approve of the length of Alfie's shirt worn by Jane Asher, nor the amount of leg exposed in that particular scene.

As a result, before they shot the scene, the wardrobe department had to cut one of Michael Caine's spare shirts of the same design and add about one foot to the length of the original one. With the shirt now reaching well below Jane Asher's knees, Victorian standards of modesty were restored. The next day, Paul McCartney came on set for inspection and stayed until the whole scene was shot. Once it had his approval, the crew moved on to the next sequence of the film.

The more melancholic part in the story was played by Vivien Merchant, who comes to visit her husband in the next bed to Alfie while he's recovering from tuberculosis in a nursing home. The chance meeting between the wife and Alfie leads to the most painful scene in the film. At a later stage, when Alfie is gradually convalescing from tuberculosis, he offers a lift to the husband's wife, which she accepts. Alfie stops the car by the river. It's a beautiful summer's day, and the two go for a row in a boat, and he seduces her again. This time will be fatal, given that she comes to his flat pregnant some weeks later.

But Alfie convinces her to abort the baby, so he summons an abortionist to his flat. But actually, the abortionist doesn't perform the abortion. He induces it, not that Alfie knows that. He's off walking with a friend because he hates all that stuff and only discovers on his return that everything is yet to come. All the doctor will say to him as he leaves is, "Two tablets if she sweats." Which doesn't sound very reassuring.

Alfie has no idea what is going to happen next. Suddenly, the wife convulses with pain. She can't stop herself from crying out. Alfie puts his hand over her mouth. Even then, he can only think of his own safety. If the neighbours were to hear and investigate, he would go to jail. The pain gets worse. The wife starts to scream, and Alfie, now in total panic, hits her across the face.

At this moment, Vivien Merchant turns to the director and the crew, telling them that she wouldn't be able to find the right reaction unless Michael Caine really hits her in the face. Michael Caine and Lewis Gilbert, the director, were uneasy about this, but they reluctantly agreed for the sake of the scene, which once on film would be there forever. Vivien started to scream again. The slap, when it came, was fearful. The wife is silenced by the shock of it but only for a moment. Then a moment later her screams grew worse and worse until, when exhausted, she eventually stopped, and the director shouted, “Cut.” The entire crew applauded.

The morning after they filmed the scene of the slap, the phone rang. It was Harold Pinter. He wanted to know what the hell they were up to on the film set, given his wife had a swollen black eye and a bruise across her face. Hadn’t Michael Caine heard of something called acting he said. Slaps are to be faked. To which Lewis Gilbert replied, “Harold, your wife asked Michael for the slap.” Then he went on, “She couldn’t play the scene otherwise, and when you see it, even though Vivien is your wife, you will say that is the most incredible piece of acting, and you will be very proud of her.”

The filming finished within less than four months, and the London premiere took place at the Plaza in Lower Regent Street, Paramount’s showcase cinema. The Beatles, the Rolling Stones and Barbara Streisand – who was able to be there because she was rehearsing the London production of *Funny Girl* – were among those who attended, which was remarkable since this was the only time the two bands were seen together at a London premiere. *Alfie* was a huge success at the box office and a huge success in the states as well, launching a new Hollywood career for Michael Caine.

Most of the film was shot on location, and the very first shoot took place at night on the Embankment, near the statue of Boudicca opposite Big Ben. Lewis Gilbert and Michael Caine decided to bring the camera in very close and have him speak, not to an audience, but to one close confidant. The intimacy of this worked so well with those who watched the rushes that they decided to keep it this way, allowing Michael Caine to speak to the audience, even though he was still on screen with another actor – who, presumably, could not hear what he was saying.

He could also make asides to the audience. In the scene with actress Eleanor Bron as the doctor who is examining Alfie for tuberculosis, on the advice of the director Lewis Gilbert, Michael Caine did the whole scene looking directly to the camera, with asides to the character on screen, turning it into one of the best scenes in *Alfie*. It set a new standard for future films to adopt the same tactic for actors to engage with the audience by talking directly to the camera, such as *Annie Hall* (1977), *American Psycho* (2000), and *Fight Club* (1999).

The song 'What's it all about, Alfie?' by Burt Bacharach and Hal David was composed and ready just before the release of *Alfie*. Both composers had singers in mind to sing it, and a few of them were offered the chance. Among them was Sandie Shaw, who already had a UK number one with one of their own compositions, 'There's always Something There To Remind Me' (1964), as well as 'Long Live Love'. She later on went on to be the first British person to win the Eurovision Song Contest with 'Puppet on a String' in 1967. Dusty Springfield also had a number four UK hit with one of Bacharach/David's compositions with 'I just Don't Know What to do with Myself' (1964), and another song by Mike Hawker, 'I Only Want To Be With You' (1963). Thereafter, she went on to have many more UK big hits with 'You Don't Have To Say You Love Me' (1966), 'Son of Preacher Man' (1968), and 'I Close My Eyes And Count To Ten', establishing her as a Swinging Sixties icon.

However, after much consideration with the Paramount bosses, they asked Cilla Black to sing it for the British release. Cilla Black had already left quite an impression on the producers of *Alfie*, with two of her songs topping the UK charts at number one: 'Anyone Who Had a Heart' and 'You're My World', both released in 1964. After the title song 'Alfie' was released, football fans would often chant it at Alf Ramsay, who was at the time the manager of the England football team. If anything went wrong, the crowds would chant, "What's it all about, Alfie?" He went on to win the world cup with the England football team, the same year as *Alfie* was released: 1966.

V. STROLL ON

For a few years in the 1960s, London was the world capital of cool. *Time* magazine dedicated its 15 April 1966 issue to London, calling it 'the Swinging City'. The article cemented the association between London and all things hip and fashionable that had been growing in the popular imagination throughout the decade. It was written by Piri Halasz, capturing the mood of the city's 'ancient elegance and new opulence... all tangled up in a dazzling blur of op and pop'. It particularly drew the attention of another giant of European cinema to come and make a film in London at the height of the Swinging Sixties: Michelangelo Antonioni.

In 1966, British film producers Jimmy Fraser and Jimmy Woolf succeeded in completing a deal for Terence Stamp on the Antonioni film, which was to be financed by Metro Goldwyn Mayer and entitled *Blow-Up*. The terms were finalised at a meeting at Jimmy Woolf's apartment with James Frazer and MGM's attorney, Lee Steiner, present. Terence Stamp was in the men's club at Les Ambassadeurs later that evening when James Woolf called him to lay out his terms and get his approval, to which he eagerly agreed, and shooting was due to start soon.

Terence Stamp borrowed a camera from his then partner, the model Jean Shrimpton. This laid the foundation for Terence Stamp to begin practising his impersonation of a Swinging Sixties photographer. Antonioni had originally written *Blow-Up* for him, given his close association with top society photographers at the time, so this was key for him to play the role in the film.

Finally, a few meetings were arranged between the Italian director Antonioni, his assistant, Claude, and the supposed leading actor for the film, Terence Stamp, during which the storyline was only discussed up to a certain point. One of Antonioni's peculiarities on this film was to keep the second half of the film a secret for personal reasons, which were never disclosed. A copy of the mysterious script was not forthcoming, but actress Joanna Shimkus was also approached to play an enigmatic female lead by the producers of the film.

Close to when the shooting was due to start, and Terence Stamp was anticipating more information on his role in *Blow-Up*, Antonioni's assistant, Claude Watson, contacted him, not to tell him that were looking forward to working with him but to break the news that Antonioni had changed his mind and had decided to cast an unknown actor called David Hemmings.

Antonioni had just seen this unknown actor in a play – *Woman in A Dressing Gown* – and was blown away by his performance, believing he was the epitome of the sixties. He was only given 14 pages of the script throughout the filming of what was originally called *A Girl, A Photographer, and an April Morning*. It was about a photographer, fed up with the fashion shoots, pot-fuelled parties, and loud music concerts of Swinging London, who goes off in search of fresh air – and fresh mischief. He plans to explore landscapes in a park but faces the enigma of a suspicious dead body under a bush, but he hasn't got his camera to capture it. So he goes back the next day to the same park and, to his surprise, the body is not there anymore. Instead, he watches a mime troupe perform an imaginary tennis match; as he watches the mime, the sound of the ball is heard, and his image fades away.

The role wasn't particularly based on one photographer, David Bailey, who shot the 'Swinging Sixties' as has been said before. David Hemmings, on Antonioni's instructions, based his character on an amalgamation of characters, with a lot of research on other society photographers, among them David Montgomery and John Cowan. In the end, the latter's persona and mannerisms during his photoshoots were instrumental to David Hemming's shaping of the character for what Antonioni had in mind. The main location of the film was filmed inside John Cowan's studio in Notting Hill. His studio was, of course, tweaked, readjusted and redesigned to serve the purpose of the film. Antonioni, prior to the filming, spent almost a year researching every aspect of photographers' lives.

While researching the background for the film, Antonioni began to appear at top fashion shoots, catwalks and even social events, adding to the ideas he already had in his mind. Quietly sitting in the background, watching models and photographers all over London, always like a shadow in the background, very much thinking and ticking along, taking the ideas.

All the forensic details of what photographers did during their photoshoots with their models were crafted meticulously, from the purple background paper to the propeller purchased by David Hemming's character for eight pounds at the fashionable Chelsea antique shop on the King's Road, to the wonderful glimpses of London. There is a scene when the photographer, Thomas, is driving through a south London street which Antonioni chose to have painted red specifically for the film: Sikhs with purple turbans and white-robed nuns watching on, all of these underlying elements capturing the evocative power that photographers had for visuals in the sixties.

Vanessa Redgrave was also asked by Antonioni to play a role in his new film, *Blow-Up*, since she was known for being part of the 'swinging' set. She began filming by day while playing every night at Wyndham theatre in *The Prime of Miss Jean Brodie* with two matinees a week. Antonioni asked her to dye her hair black and shave it an inch from her hairline to give her a higher forehead.

Antonioni told *Blow-Up*'s story through the camera angle, its movement, the frame, the objects in the frame, their colour, position and movement, whether human or inanimate. The dialogue was of no great significance or certainly of secondary importance. As a trained dancer, she was able to appreciate this, and she learned to look sharply and precisely at the shapes and colours around her.

Vanessa Redgrave's exact positions, angles of the body, head and shoulders, and exact tempo of movement were vital to Antonioni on the film set to the point that she had never encountered such an eye for perfection in the cinema. In English and American films, colours and shapes were part of the decoration, appropriate, but only as background to the action.

Blow-Up was about the unity and difference of essence and phenomena; the conflict between what is, objectively, seen, heard or grasped by the individual. Antonioni's ear, not for dialogue but for the sounds of nature and normally inanimate objects, was as subtle as his eye. The sound of the leaves rustling in that park scene set in Maryon Park is mesmerising. Antonioni thought the roads and fences were a bit grey in Maryon Park and had them painted black, as well as the protagonist's car, which was originally a red Rolls Royce belonging to Jimmy Saville. Moreover, it was said that even pigeons were dyed, so they were just the right sort of pigeons.

In another scene, Hemmings watches a group of carefree students silently miming a game of tennis in the park. When they hit their imaginary ball out of the court, he picks it up and throws it back. It makes one wonder whether the murder was all in his mind. Was, to some certain degree, the Swinging Sixties anything more than a fleeting collective hallucination? Antonioni, in one scene, might have summed up the mood of Swinging London; one's state of mind. He later admitted that he chose to shoot the film in London because there was a particular sort of social phenomenon there that was livelier, freer, more advanced and extreme than anywhere else, including Paris, Rome, or New York.

The award-winning Michelangelo Antonioni's monumental film was the only film to date capturing the whole essence and energy of Swinging London. *Blow-Up* was premiered on 14 December 1966 in London and went on general release. After the premiere, a sort of event was organised to see the film with the crew and was attended by the Yardbirds, who, apart from the section they had recorded, knew very little about the film. The production team seemed to know as little about the plot as anyone else involved with the film did. *Blow-Up* was the first film to have shown naked teenage models, though the unadorned breasts and drug-fuelled parties were not as explicit in the final version of the film, given it underwent a censorship process by the British Board of Film Censors.

At the time of the premiere in New York, it was said that Antonioni was asked what the 'blow-up' was during the shoot, and he replied, "This is the blow-up," referring to the guitar-breaking scene carried out by the members of the Yardbirds. Jeff Beck was asked directly by Antonioni to smash his guitar, which was a Hofner brand, in emulation of the Who's Pete Townshend – who smashed his guitar at the end of performing their 1965 UK and US hit song 'My Generation'. Their scene in the film was shot at Elstree Studios in Borehamwood, where Antonioni had a set built that was an authentic replica of the Ricky Tick Club at Clewer Mead in Windsor.

For *Blow-Up*, the Yardbirds recorded the track 'Stroll On' at IBC studios in London. It was the first time Jeff Beck and Jimmy Page got to record with the guitars. The song was a reworking of Tiny Bradshaw's 'Train Kept A-Rollin', having changed the song's lyrics and title to avoid having to seek permission from the copyright holder. The Who, In-Crowd and the Velvet Underground were Antonioni's first choice, respectively, but were unable to attend the filming. The Yardbirds were topping the charts in 1966 with their avant-garde rock psychedelic single, 'Happenings Ten Years' Time Ago', which seemed to have impressed Antonioni and influenced his decision to approach them for *Blow-Up*.

The alternative premiere in London was also attended by Veruschka, a famous model of the time and muse to Helmut Newton, who featured in the film.After the end of the screening, she was almost reduced to tears when she saw that her five days' work on the film set was reduced to only 30 seconds at the party scene and was cut ruthlessly in the editing room by the director, Michelangelo Antonioni.

The latter is believed to have not been happy with Veruschka during her time on the set. David Hemmings says to Veruschka at a party in scenes 47–49, “I thought you were meant to be in Paris!”

She stonily replies, “I am in Paris.”

It was shot at the designer Christopher Gibbs’ house next to the Thames on 100 Cheyne Walk, and the party scene took just over five days to film.

One of the reasons the party scene took so long to film was that Veruschka, most of the time, really was in Paris and took a taxi to London. She was severely delayed for that famous party scene, which, despite the camera running for about five days solid, ended up about 30 seconds long. It seems Michelangelo had still not forgiven Veruschka for her unpunctuality. Veruschka’s part of lead model was originally offered to Twiggy. But Antonioni’s demands for her to pose naked while lying on the floor during the photo shoot with the main protagonist, Thomas, prompted her to decline to appear in the film.

Twiggy was not the only model who had reservations about how the film treated the models. At the beginning of the film, there is a studio fashion shoot session in which David Hemmings’s character is photographing five models: Jill Kennington, Peggy Moffit, Rosaleen Murray, Ann Norman, and Melanie Hampshire.

The clothes and wardrobes from the fashion shoot sequence were mostly selections from Mary Quant’s various fashion shows. Antonioni was present at every single of them in the run-up to the filming of *Blow-Up*, with some of the clothes designed for that specific sequence by Jocelyne Rickards. Despite this, Veruschka preferred to bring and wear her own clothes on the set of *Blow-Up* for that party sequence at the end of the film. Once that scene got underway, one of the models, Jill Kennington, felt uncomfortable because she was asked to be as stiff and formal as a shop window mannequin, which she found absurd and alien to her usual working ethos while posing for John Cowan and other prominent sixties photographers. Although she was grateful for being cast in the film, she was discontented about that aspect during the filming in April 1966.

Furthermore, Jane Birkin, an Ossie Clarke model, seemingly shocked the audience when it was first released in December 1966 because of her on-screen promiscuity: being half-naked and showing her pubic hair, and distinguishing herself by becoming the first British actress to show her pubic hair in a non-sex film. Retrospectively, all these aspects of the film might have contributed to its phenomenal success, with critics calling it an ambiguous and fascinating film, grossing £20 million at the box office worldwide against a backdrop of its £1.8 million budget. *Blow-Up* went on to win Palme d'Or at the Cannes Film Festival that year, becoming the second Swinging London film ever to have won it, the other being *The Knack ...and How to Get It* (1965). Apart from its promiscuity, which it had in common with *Blow-Up,* it also featured a young Jane Birkin in her film debut.

VI. TIME OF THE SEASON

The mid-summer of 1966 was the apogee of London's happy, optimistic, golden age turned into a dreamland. Hyde Park had become a hive of activity. Pop concerts and art galleries were on every corner you would have imagined. The Indica Gallery and Robert Fraser's gallery were revelling in the outbreak of positive feeling and the explosion of style and colour that was dubbed the 'Swinging Sixties' by *Time* magazine.

The gallery owner Robert Fraser was instrumental as the art director in getting *Sgt. Pepper's Lonely Hearts Club Band* album cover together and getting Peter Blake involved with the design. He was also responsible for the Indica Gallery's 1966 Yoko Ono exhibition, where her installations were dangling from the ceiling, and where she met John Lennon when he was still a member of the Beatles. He also inspired the Beatles' record company by leaving a Magritte painting of an apple on the Beatles' kitchen table, resulting in the name Apple.

Bazaar, Granny Takes a Trip, Hung On You and Gandalf's Garden boutiques on the King's Road, while rivalling one another, were nonetheless revolutionising the world's ready-to-wear by turning London into a catwalk for fashion revellers. Heralding a new fashion of Swinging London: vintage clothes, floral chiffon shirts and high-buttoned Mao jackets, which encapsulated and captured the psychedelic mood of that time.

Men adopted dandy looks in coloured Victorian frock coats with ruffles and floral ties, and women wore 'Fuz' or 'Koko' sunglasses designed by Oliver Goldsmith, which were trendsetters by Emma Peel in *The Avengers* series. Miniskirts with knee-high Biba boots or space-age boots, velvet trousers, Victorian bustles, Edwardian Charleston robes, floppy black or helmet hats were in, while mod snazziness, and the beatnik fashion often seen on Carnaby street were on the way out. Britain was heading for the 'new heat of the technological revolution'; the new establishment, as they were called, were adopting a retrograde of Victorian/Edwardian fashion and lifestyle to defy the will of the 'old establishment'.

The fashionable look of the time was by Leigh Lawson, later known as Twiggy or Twigs. She often wore an iconic Biba dress: A-line with a tight top and little armholes, the hem two inches above the knee. It had a primrose-yellow background with a pink one-inch chevron pattern in zigzag and gingham phases. It had a high neck and puff sleeves to the elbow, with three round pearl buttons at the neck, encompassing the Swinging London spirits and colours.

Teenagers would also have their hair cut short, copying the hairstyle of Twiggy. Twiggy was named by the *Daily Express* as 'the face of 1966' when, in January of that year, she was discovered by photographer Lewis Morley – who was known for the provocative nude photos of Christine Keeler sitting in a chair – while having gone on a stroll with her boyfriend, Justine De Villeneuve.

Another great figure emerging from the Swinging Sixties was a muse to Salvador Dali, Amanda Lear, also the subject of the Rolling Stones' song 'Miss Amanda Jones', who was to model Ossie Clarke's collection at the Revolution nightclub in the summer of 1966. The day before the collection was due to happen, she went to Quorum boutique in Radnor Walk in Chelsea for a fitting where Ossie Clarke and his wife, Celia Birtwell, also a fashion designer, worked and made clothes. Colourful floral shirts, white flared Venetian cloth, and flapper dresses were all part of Ossie Clarke's collection that year. The courtiers on that magnificent occasion included the Beatles, Pattie Boyd, Brian Jones, and Marianne Faithfull. Terence Stamp, Donyale Luna with her gold-tinted contact lenses, David Hockney, and all the fashionable photographers made it one of the most memorable collections, which defined that era by its opulence, extravagance, and decadence.

The British social scene, with its centuries of tradition, was changing almost beyond recognition. Although Mick Jagger, still with Marianne Faithfull, was a key figure, Brian Jones, with Anita Pallenberg on his arm, was becoming a far more flamboyant symbol of the new, exotic pop aristocracy. The old aristocracy had a sense of entitlement, of continuity. There was none of that now.

A veritable microcosm of the 1960s British society is meticulously captured in photographer Gered Mankowitz's iconic photo session with the Yardbirds. It was shot in the autumn of 1966, just outside his Ormond Yard studio situated behind Piccadilly Circus. In the background there was the symbol of the British establishment striding past, wearing his bowler hat, looking toward the camera, snapped between the legs of the lead singer Keith Relf, reflecting the social change that was taking place. But also framed by the Relf thighs appeared to be a working man in overalls and flat cap walking towards the establishment figure.

Furthermore, London was becoming the capital of a unique moment in modern culture, dazzling with opulence, elegance and sheer magnetism. One specific film was to capture all that experimentation, promiscuity and permissiveness: *Georgy Girl.* Based on a novel and co-written by Margaret Forster with Peter Nicholas, who had previously written the script for a successful Swinging London musical called *Catch Us If You Can,* featuring the Dave Clark Five. Pre-marital sex, promiscuity, sleeping with your pregnant friend's husband, and discussing abortion casually were not popular themes with the British Board of Film Censors went it first went into production; they called the script immoral, edgy, and scandalous.

It tells the story of a virginal young woman called Georgy Parkin, played by Lynn Redgrave, during

Swinging Sixties London. She is acquiescent and acquisitive, but that soon changes when she begins sharing a flat with saucy, pleasure-seeking and promiscuous Meredith (Charlotte Rampling) through whom she meets Meredith's boyfriend, Jos (Alan Bates). But soon after they get married and Meredith becomes pregnant, Jos indulges in an affair with Georgy, his wife's flatmate. As the affair is discovered by Meredith, and also given the latter is driven by self-obsessed selfishness, she takes off, leaving the baby behind her. Georgy's intense liking for domesticity becomes apparent when it seems Georgy cares more for the baby than for having an adult relationship with Jos. Jos leaves both the baby and Georgy to pursue a new life, with social services attempting to remove the baby from her care.

As she's facing a dilemma in her life, humour is added to the film largely from Georgy's other life, in which her parents are housekeepers to a middle-aged northern millionaire, Mr James, played by James Mason. Unbeknownst to her parents, Georgy has become the object of desire for their employer, who pursues her with a touch of comic desperation. He was unable to express his true feelings for Georgy while his wife was still alive, but now she is deceased, he finds himself free to express his love for her, so he proposes marriage with Georgy accepting it as it will allow her to keep baby Sara by adopting her.

The last scene, which is the wedding day, was filmed at Chelsea Town Hall on the King's Road, which was, in the 1960s, part of London's social scene. Due to James Mason's busy filming schedule for other productions, this had to be shot in the first three weeks, and then they filmed the other scenes featured at the beginning of the film, including the ones with Charlotte Rampling and Alan Bates. Lynn Redgrave also asked for her mum, Rachel Kempson, to play her on-screen husband's wife, Mrs Leamington, who suddenly dies halfway through the film.

The title song, written by Tom Springfield and Jim Dale, was recorded by an Australian band, the Seekers, which pushed the film to greater success by topping the charts in the United Kingdom, United States, Canada, and Australia. It earned the film an academy award nomination for best original song from a motion picture category; the other two nominations were in the best supporting actor category by James Mason and best cinematography – black and white – by Kenneth Higgins.

It's also important to note that the director Silvio Narizzano's first choice was Vanessa Redgrave as the leading lady, who he believed was the beautiful Greta Garbo of the Swinging Sixties, but she had already committed herself to another film. Therefore, she passed the role on to her sister, Lynn, who made quite an impression on the director by making her character wear unflattering clothes and having messy hair throughout the filming. She embodied the characteristics of Georgy, who, although immoral, ruthless and unconventional, her appeal to the teenagers of her era is important: she's a survivor. Lynn Redgrave earned *Georgy Girl* one of its four nominations at the Academy Awards in the best actress category, but lost it to Elizabeth Taylor for *Who's Afraid of Virginia Woolf?* Another fellow nominee on that night was her sister, Vanessa, for another film, *Morgan – A Suitable Case For Treatment,* for which she had, in fact, declined *Georgy Girl.* This prompted that year's Academy Awards' master of the ceremony, actor and comedian Bob Hope, to make a quip about the Redgrave family: "All the world's a stage and the Redgraves are merely players."

Meanwhile, a new generation of affluent young people was attracting back independent filmmakers such as Karel Reisz, Tony Richardson, and Ken Loach. Those stalwarts of Free Cinema spearheaded a style of filmmaking that was light on frills, spending the beginning of the 1960s up in the north. Thanks to the work of playwrights and authors like John Osborne, Harold Pinter and Neil Dunn, these films brought on-screen depictions of class division and urban life deteriorated by the futilities of bomb-damaged and drained Britannia during the Blitz years as well as the transformation of a new England, now becoming the heartland of a new wave.

In the same year as *Georgy Girl*, Vanessa Redgrave had decided to join Karel Reisz, the director of *Saturday Night and Sunday Morning*, now embarking on his nearest approximation to a Swinging London film in *Morgan – A Suitable Case For Treatment.*

She played the role of Leonie Delt, whose husband, Morgan, was played by David Warner in the lead role.

Morgan is about a troubled, impossible misfit from a traditional, working-class background who is obsessed with Karl Marx and gorillas, and is married to his well-to-do Kensington-born upper-class wife, played by Vanessa Redgrave. She is despairing of her marriage to him and is seeking a divorce in order to marry an art gallery owner (Robert Stephens) from her own social standing. Prevented by a court injunction from approaching her, the main protagonist, Morgan, dons a gorilla suit in order to exact a King Kong revenge on the society he blames for his predicament. His psychological and political confusion is sublimated into an obsession with a gorilla.

Reisz's investment of some fellow feeling is evident in the intensity with which Morgan's suffering and fantasy is presented as a surreal expression of character while usurping social realism. Morgan is constantly indulged in his revenge as he crashes the wedding reception of his ex-wife in his gorilla suit, as well as the muddled set of political references that underpin it: his allegiance to communism and obsession with Karl Marx. This seemed at odds with the consumerist society that Britain was becoming by 1966, which was also reflective of Karel Weisz's own views in his youth. Morgan, an outcast in the urban wilderness, embodied Weisz's theory of how society breaks the non-conformists during Swinging London. The battle between Leonie and Morgan is finally resolved when Leonie visits Morgan in an insane asylum to tell him she is pregnant with his baby, the scene at which the film ends.

Another film that captured the unattractive part of London during the Swinging Sixties was *Poor Cow* by a new upcoming director, Ken Loach. He had already established a reputation for realism and for the technique of using improvisation in *Cathy Come Home*. He cast, once again, Carol White as the lead and focus of the entire film, who he had previously worked with on *Cathy Come Home,* a TV play which depicts the story of a British woman who faces a downward social climb thanks to the unfairness of the welfare system.

Poor Cow is a highly politicised film about a young working-class mother living in London who embarks on a number of tumultuous relationships. Often this is with criminals, including Tom (Terence Stamp), with whom she shares a daughter, and Dave (Johnny Bindon), with whom she indulges in an affair while Tom serves time in prison for robbery. But once Dave is imprisoned for 12 years for leading a robbery, resulting in a woman becoming blind, she drifts into promiscuity with other men. However, once her child's father, Tom (Terence Stamp), gets released, she decides to raise their child together despite the domestic abuse she sometimes has to deal with and his abusive temperament. Although living in poverty in the slums and mistreated by her lovers, Joy remains resilient about her lot. This was the second

Ken Loach production regarding society's treatment of the working-class during Swinging London.

But unlike *Cathy Come Home*, which was adapted from a play, it did not have a script. It was one of the interesting aspects of the film, which was wholly improvised. Although Ken Loach did not have a script and merely had the idea, he also had the overall trajectory in his mind. Consequently, sequences had to be taken in one because each of the actors had a camera on them. Before a scene was shot, Ken Loach would say something to Carol White and then something completely different to Terence Stamp, and they would only discover once the camera was rolling that he had given both his leading actors two different directions resulting in confusion and spontaneity.

This occurred when there was a scene between Carol White and Terence Stamp, in which Joy threw stew over her boyfriend, Dave, without Terence Stamp being aware of it. As a result, he had to go off the set and buy himself new clothes and come back again wearing them, given his old ones had already been ruined.

The film was set between Battersea and Clapham Junction, which is a world away from psychedelia or Swinging London. The writer, Nell Dunn, whose book inspired Ken Loach to make the film, actually set her stories south of the river. Ken Loach decided to cast a real-life part of the London underworld, Johnny Bindon, who had served time in prison prior to the filming, as Carol White's on-screen husband.

Furthermore, the film is more focused on the criminal underclass of London and set among the lower class – the so-called underdog – which is in contrast to the other side of the river where Swinging London is happening. But certainly, the Swinging Sixties style is not something the main protagonist Joy can aspire to, as she has to make do with cheap dolly dresses and plastic knee boots from the market. Furthermore, London always had that divide between 'Up West' versus the East End and South of the River. In one scene, Joy and her friend, Beryl, gaze at two 60s women dressed like 'dolly birds' and comment ruefully about how young they look, although they would be the same age. But Ken Loach masterfully used that scene to evoke the social rifts that were crippling (in his view) London society at the time; the audience can distinguish them from one another, given they're simply a world apart.

Nonetheless, there are still a few conspicuous Swinging London themes in the film: most of the songs heard in the film were written by Donovan, musician, songwriter, and record producer, mostly revolving around his arrest in the mid-sixties when he became the first high-profile British pop star to be arrested for the possession of cannabis. This was at a party which was rumoured to be attended by the Rolling Stones' Mick Jagger, the Who's Pete Townshend, and Cream's Ginger Baker. Among the songs performed by Donovan in *Poor Cow* are the title song, 'Be Not Too Hard', and, 'Colours', with the latter sung by the character played by Terence Stamp.

The other 60s theme relates to Joy, played by Carol White. After taking a job as a barmaid, Joy starts modelling for a seedy photographers' club and drifts into promiscuity. This echoes the relationships that the Swinging Sixties' photographers had at that time with their models/muses, including Duffy with Celia Hammond, John Cowan with Jill Kennington, and, the most prominent of them all, David Bailey's much-publicised relationship with Jean Shrimpton, lasting four years.

And, lastly, the sexual freedom that Carol White's character, Joy, has dominates the narrative. Throughout the film, there is more about her experiences, thoughts on men and sexual adventures in a free-flowing, ungrammatical stream, thanks to the contraceptive pill in the 1960s, allowing women to have greater sexual freedom and control over their own bodies. As in the book, Joy embarks on a string of sexual encounters with a baker, a butcher, a sailor, a hairdresser, a professor, a watchmaker, and a photographer while on a stint as a glamour model in a studio on the North End Road, seeking sexual experiences compulsively rather than in pursuit of pleasure. However, this was a world of change – senses in overload, meters running into the red – a potent example of the insecurity and volatility of the London scene, culminating in a new film called *Privilege*.

VII. WATERLOO SUNSET

As Britain drifted into 1967, the British cultural scene boomed across Europe and, in particular, in the United States. The British Invasion was at the top of its success. There also seemed a lot of attention focused on the sheer magnetism of London. The Rolling Stones' *Between the Buttons* album cover was taken in St. James' Park at the centre of all London attractions, the Beatles' *Sgt. Pepper's Lonely Hearts Club Band* encompassed all the underlying themes reflected within Swinging London society at the time: psychedelic imagery, contemporary youth, and the counterculture. And lastly, the Kinks, with their 'Waterloo Sunset' single featured on their *Something Else* album, was a love letter to London.

It also pays homage to Terence Stamp and Julie Christie: "Terry meets Julie, Waterloo Station every Friday night", reflecting the romantic relationship between the two in 1967 on the set of *Far From The Madding Crowd*, who both became the apogee of Swinging Sixties London. Subsequently, more attention was drawn to the British film industry in 1967 from pop idols to the extent that some of them gave up their career to become full-time actors, including English singer, Paul Jones.

In the early summer of 1967, the model, Jean Shrimpton, was approached about making a film called *Privilege*. This was a package being put together by John Heyman and Peter Watkins, one of Heyman's clients, who was to be the director. Paul Jones, the heart-throb pop star, the frontman of the pop band Manfred Mann, who were leading in the UK singles chart with number-one songs such as: 'Do Wah Diddy Diddy', 'Pretty Flamingo', and 'Mighty Quinn', before leaving the band to pursue a film career.

Now, he was playing his first lead role in a feature film, and there had also been talk of Sarah Miles as his co-star. Sarah Miles was already signed up to play in *Blow-Up*; therefore, Jean Shrimpton was signed up instead with no acting experience. Jean Shrimpton had reservations about the role, given she was adamant she could not act and walking on catwalks was a mile apart from appearing in a film.

On the other hand, Peter Watkins, the director, was a serious filmmaker. He had never made a big expensive film, but his work on *The War Game* and *Culloden* – both low-budget films – had received strong critical acclaim. She put her trust in him, given she felt that he had a credible reputation.

It was arranged for the director, Peter Watkins, and Jean Shrimpton to meet, with the latter conscious that Peter really wanted Sarah Miles for the part. He already had one untried actor in Paul Jones, so it was not surprising that he was uncertain about coping with two of them. As it happened, Peter Watkins rather fell for Jean Shrimpton in a quiet way, and despite his original resistance to casting her for the part, surprisingly, he gave in and said he would make the film with her.

Although Jean Shrimpton got along well with her co-star Paul Jones, she did not enjoy making *Privilege*, battling her way through the film, forcing herself to go to the studio every day. However, the experience of the film filled in time and kept her away from her then boyfriend and established her independence from anyone having an influence on her life.

The premiere was at the Prince of Wales cinema near Albany in Piccadilly, near where Jean Shrimpton and Terence Stamp resided. As Terence Stamp was away filming *Modesty Blaise* in Italy with Monica Vitti, his brother, Chris, who was managing the Who at the time, volunteered to join her. Keith Richards and Anita Pallenberg, the golden couple of that era, were also present, blindsided by the flashes of the cameras following them wherever they went, with Anita wearing a gold sequin dress and Keith wearing a white kaftan shirt.

At the showing of the film, Jean Shrimpton famously squirmed lower in her seat every time she appeared on the screen. Alexander Walker, the prominent *London Evening Standard* film critic, wrote: “she looked as if she had been directed by an anaesthetist”. Another insisted that she “should stick to getting on and off planes”. After coming under fire for her acting in the film, Jean Shrimpton rather found the result of that disaster hard to live with, resulting in her withdrawing from the scene and even considering retirement from the public arena.

Nonetheless, there was one bonus that came from making *Privilege*. In the script, the girl she played was originally meant to be a journalist, but Peter Watkins decided that no way would she ever be convincing as a newspaper woman, so he changed the character to a painter. That decision expanded the start Jean Shrimpton had at the Colombe d'Or in the South of France in opening her eyes to art. Peter Watkins wanted her to take painting lessons so that at least she held the brush correctly. She wished now she had been more diligent about the lessons, but she did learn something.

The man who was teaching her had a catalogue of Egon Schiele's work. She had never heard of Egon Schiele at that point, an incredible draughtsman who had died when he was only 28. He and his wife both died in the flu epidemic of 1918 – an epidemic that killed more people than the First World War itself. She looked at these productions of his paintings and felt the tug that something of remarkable strength and beauty brings. She was enthralled.

They were pictures of emaciated people and objects, full of power and strange eroticism. She found them unforgettable, and they were very much in her consciousness for days. She was talking to Desmond Fitzgerald, the Knight of Glin, who worked at Sotheby's, about the effect they had had on her, and he said, "The Marlborough Gallery has some of Schiele's work if you are that interested." She went straight there and bought two of his pictures. They were expensive, but nothing compared with what they are worth now – not that she owns them anymore. And from then on, she began to develop an interest in buying pictures.

As 'the Swinging City', London was once more a Mecca as an international symbol of cultural upheaval as well as a draw for filmmakers, but this time it was Michael Winner's turn to take the lead with his next film: *I'll Never Forget What's'isname*. The film is about a young man in advertising who goes to work, smashes up his desk with an axe, and decides to return to the simple life: Swinging London. It dealt with themes that, in retrospect, are highly significant, such as pollution, the desire to get out of the rat race, and man's inability to come to terms with an increasingly complex and industrialised world. It featured a sarcastic and witty chief of an advertising job, played by Oliver Reed.

For one of Oliver Reed's girlfriends, Michael Winner chose Marianne Faithfull, who was regarded in 1967 as the harlot of Britain. She had been involved in various sexual shenanigans and was having a much-publicised relationship in the press at that time with the Rolling Stones' Mick Jagger. Jagger was at the height of his bad boy period with his band peeing on the ground in petrol stations which would put them on the other end of the spectrum compared to the Beatles. She went to see Michael Winner at his offices wearing a white trouser suit with a wide-brimmed white hat. After the audition was over, she spent the entire time apologising, saying she hoped she wasn't embarrassing him by being too outrageously dressed in Swinging London flamboyant dresses. He thought the opposite, that she was dressed in a nice and simple manner.

The leading girl in *I'll Never Forget What's'isname* was Carol White, who had previously debuted in *Poor Cow,* which was still in post-production. Although she seemed to have juggled this rather well, going back and forth, doing both productions. During the course of the filming, Carol started an affair with Oliver Reed while being married to her husband, Mike. Their affair lasted throughout the shooting of the film, despite both of them being married and Oliver Reed having a child. They used to meet up at Michael Winner's flat in the evening after a busy day on set and, to his surprise, ask him to leave his flat, so they could have their intimacy there, and he duly obliged.

I'll Never Forget What's'isname had a wonderful cast, including Orson Welles, Harry Andrews, Michael Hordern, Wendy Craig, Frank Finlay, Edward Fox, and Norman Rodway. The release was an enormous critical success for capturing Swinging London so compellingly in swift, funny, violent, candidly sexy, and sometimes poignant strokes that cemented the film's reputation as a towering virtue of honesty and force.

However, it caused some controversy and outrage as well: the Catholic Legion of Decency in the United

States, which at the time held some sway, decided to ban the film because of one specific sequence which implied cunnilingus. There is a scene where Oliver Reed and Carol White are on a houseboat. After a row, Carol White's character gets on the floor, and Oliver Reed disappears off-screen between her legs, and later she knocks over a pot of white paint in a fairly obvious piece of symbolism.

Author's father during the swinging sixties, the inspiration for this book.

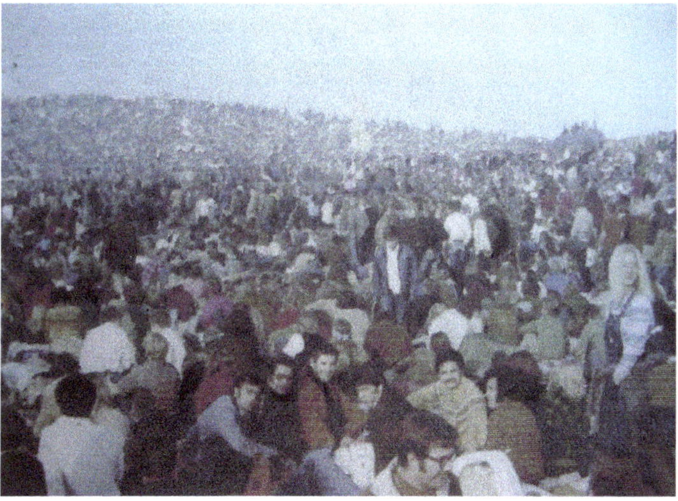

Author's father, sitting on the far right and clad in a brown sweatshirt, at the Rolling Stones' free concert - Altamont in 1969.

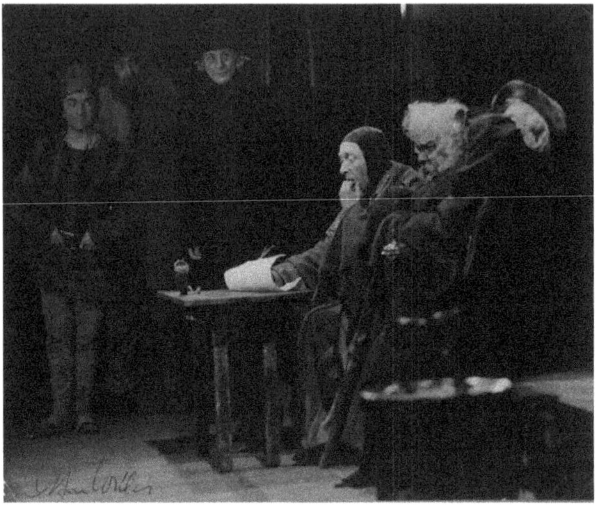

Lee Harris, standing in the middle, playing alongside the great Orson Welles during London rehearsals of Shakespeare's "Chimes at Midnight" in 1960. It was shortly before Lee Harris quit acting and became one of the Swinging Sixties' avid campaigners (inscribed by Orson Welles).

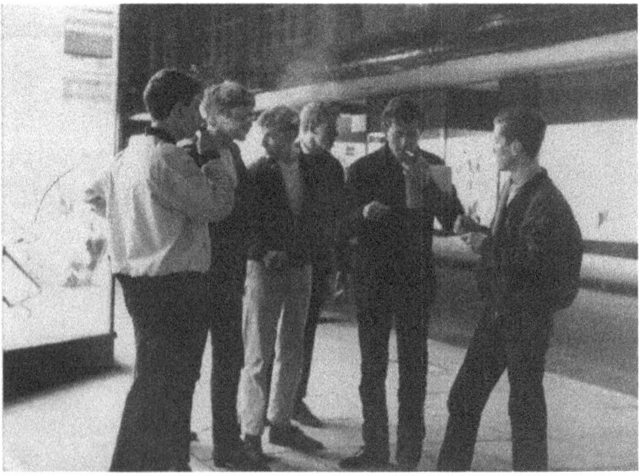

Mods in Soho, London, 1963 with actor Lee Harris (centre) smoking a cigarette.

Model Amanda Lear whose relationship with Brian Jones inspired the track "Miss Amanda Jones" by the Rolling Stones in 1967.

London 1967. Amanda Lear sporting 'psychedelic' fashion with two Beatles: John Lennon & George Harrison.

Cartoonist Gerald Scarfe's sketch titled 'Their New Incarnation' of the Beatles, featured in Time magazine's publication on 22nd September 1967, offered a whimsical and insightful portrayal of the band's evolution.

Photographer Frank Habicht immortalized a unique perspective of the Rolling Stones in the early 1960s, capturing moments of the band while they were sharing their first flat together at 102 Edith Grove in Chelsea.

Plastic Ono Band Xmas 1969 London at the Lyceum Theatre on Drury Lane in the West End, a charity concert for UNICEF. On stage were John Lennon and Yoko Ono accompanied by George Harrison.

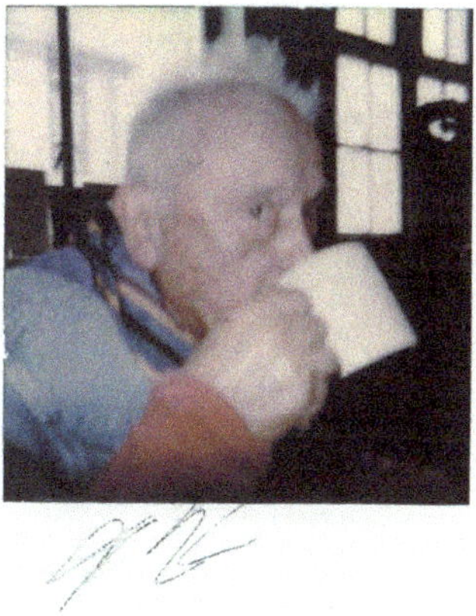

The author commemorated the 60th anniversary of Swinging Sixties photographer David Bailey's illustrious career in fashion photography by capturing a captivating portrait of him.

Sir Michael Caine attained international stardom through his unforgettable portrayal in "Alfie" (1966) directed by Lewis Gilbert, which perfectly captured the spirit of the Swinging Sixties and became a significant cultural touchstone of the era.

Julie Christie, a celebrated icon of the Swinging Sixties, who earned an Oscar for her outstanding performance in the 1965 film "Darling," directed by John Schlesinger.

During the Swinging Sixties, Sir Elton John was a session musician at Abbey Road Studios, contributing his talent to the vibrant musical scene.

Terence Stamp whose contributions to the film industry and his connection to the Swinging Sixties have left a lasting impact, making him a memorable figure in the cultural history of 1960s London.

James Fox starred in the film "Performance" (1970),
directed by Donald Cammell and Nicolas Roeg, which has
since become a cult classic associated with the Swinging Sixties.

The final interview with the late photographer Terry O'Neil, whose iconic images remarkably encapsulated the essence of the Swinging Sixties.

VIII. YOU CAN'T ALWAYS GET WHAT YOU WANT

Mick Jagger and Marianne Faithfull had just moved into a house on Cheyne Walk, which looked onto the Thames, next door to an antique dealer friend, Christopher Gibbs. Keith Richards and his girlfriend, Anita Pallenberg, lived a few yards further down the road. Not far away, on Tite Street – where Oscar Wilde once lived – was the home of David Milnaric, the fashionable interior decorator, who printed his wallpapers in dark and sombre shades. It was the fashion in those days to have these sombre interiors and rooms cluttered with antiques. David Bailey, who had just married Catherine Deneuve, had painted his entire house black, including the ceilings.

And right afterwards, the Rolling Stones' film debut came in a Jean-Luc Godard production, *One Plus One*. From their recording sessions on 4th June onwards, camera crew had moved in to film them. The Stones' role in this hundred-minute film was to act as a kind of backdrop to the story of a girl who arrived in London and freaked out. To Mick Jagger, particularly, the most important aspect of this film was the lucky break when Godard, by chance, filmed the complete evolution of the song 'Sympathy for the Devil' as it changed course over several sessions.

It began as a folky song, rather like 'Jigsaw Puzzle', but it didn't work, so they kept changing it until finally it evolved as a samba. The song was originally titled 'The Devil is My Name', but its final title, 'Sympathy for the Devil', was also used for the film's American release.

By contrast with the earlier plans for a film, this one progressed efficiently and didn't need too much of their attention. They received a fee in June 1968 of $50,000 (£18,878); a special clause in the contract recognised the difficulties of Brian Jones in relation to his arrest and protected his participation in the film: "The non-availability of Brian Jones to perform his services under the contract arising from the current charge against him shall not entitle them to suspend nor determine the artist's services thereunder".

In the meantime, the band was on a high as they made plans for their new album, *Beggars Banquet,* featuring 'Sympathy for the Devil' as its number one song on side one. There were grandiose plans for its cover, which went through many changes before ending up as simple script lettering on a white background. They hired two bays in the Cadogan Square car park for three full days from the 7th June for the purpose of painting a grand piano. The office ordered five pairs of cricket pads, stumps, bails, two balls, and two bats from the cricket firm of Jack Hobbs. From theatrical costumiers Berman and Nathan, they ordered some outlandish gear: Mick Jagger, dressed as a swell, wore trousers, top hat, a tailcoat and pumps, Charlie Watts dressed as a stable groom, wore shirt, tricorn, breeches, waistcoat, boots, and stock. The rest of them wore assorted hats, boots, cord trousers, and medieval tunics. Also on hand were black skullcaps, assorted medieval shirts, breeches, seven pairs of tights, tunics, and rough leather jerkins. The album cover picture, as they planned it, was photographed with them dressed as tramps at a house they rented in Hampstead called Satum Chase.

All-night sessions at the Olympic were the norm during the completion of the album, and the adrenalin was flowing with the presence of Godard's film crew. His method suited them perfectly, for he had no real master plan nor firm script. He worked from one point to another, filming a piece and then deciding what to do next after looking at the result. As Keith Richards pointed out, that was precisely how they shaped their songs and recording sessions. Nothing was ever firmly laid down, and songs went through many changes of structure and rhythm before completion.

Nicky Hopkins, the keyboards player, was brought in to augment the band on this album, with Glyn Johns engineering and Jimmy Miller producing. But a near-disaster left the crew shaken and almost ended Jean-Luc Godard's adventures with the Rolling Stones when the recording tapes nearly burnt when the studio was set on fire before they got retrieved and preserved in a safe place.

After an all-night session on the 10th June, the heat from the film crew's arc lamps set fire to the ceiling.

The rest of the band had left, and Bill Wyman's first thought was to save the tapes: he and Jimmy Millers dashed into the control room and then into the vaults to pull them clear, and then they ran for safety. Everyone was evacuated while three fire engines came within minutes to extinguish the blaze. Guitars, amplifiers, a Hammond organ, and photographic equipment were all soaked. After the firemen had finished, Jimmy Miller and Bill Wyman returned the undamaged tapes safely to the studio's tape vault before they left for home.

In 1967, Dirk Bogarde gave a very grand Christmas party at the Connaught Hotel, where he had his own suite from the beginning of the sixties. All the luminaries of the theatre were there: Maggie Smith, Paul Schofield, Julie Christie. Essentially all those celebrities Robin Fox represented, through whom Marianne Faithfull had just landed herself the part of Irina in *The Three Sisters* at the Royal Court alongside Glenda Jackson in a play originally written by Anton Chekov.

It was a terribly stuffy affair; the hippest person at the party was Julie Christie. You would have thought a theatrical gathering of this kind would have been bubbling with witty repartee and wicked anecdotes, but instead it was merely actors talking shop. Only in England during the 'Swinging Sixties' did the leading members of the acting profession carry on like the upper reaches of the clergy.

Across the smoky room, Marianne Faithfull kept an eye on James Fox and his new girlfriend at the time, who she knew through his father who represented her.

James Fox had already become an established actor thanks to his portrayal of the feckless upper-class character he portrayed in the film *The Servant*, and that's where his persona came from. But it was James Fox's girlfriend, Andee Cohen – very exquisite, sassy and vivacious – who first chatted with Marianne Faithfull, both having a great time, laughing and gossiping.

After that evening, they became good friends and started hanging out together with their respective partners: Mick Jagger and James Fox. It was a folie à quatre. James Fox was fascinated by Mick Jagger as if by some genie of mimicry and energy, and Mick Jagger was taken by him too, given he always had a thing for upper-class folk.

Mick Jagger's curiosity about James Fox had a professional element to it as well, given the latter was a well-established actor, and Mick Jagger had started considering acting as a possible career for himself. They would often go out and have dinner together, often to a restaurant on Fulham Road called the Baghdad House with curtained booths. The restaurant was run by two Moroccan brothers. Customers smoked hash openly in the restaurant and listened to wonderful chromatic maqam music.

The best part of their relationship with James Fox and Andee Cohen, though, were the long white nights spent lounging at each other's houses. They would go over to James Fox's flat, or they would go to Mick Jagger and Marianne Faithfull at 48 Cheyne Walk and drink wine. They were enchanted evenings;

everything unfolded with magical ease in the spirit of those times they were living in.

They sifted through the past, selecting exquisite bits and pieces from Victorian and Edwardian times: furniture, books, ideas, and art. Andee Cohen would talk effusively about her past lives, Egypt, Samaria, the court of Louis I, the Tang dynasty. Mick Jagger and Marianne Faithfull were wonderful hosts and entertained them by playing wonderful old blues and Motown, Hank and Audrey Williams duets and Smokey Robinson too, who he regarded as the godfather of soul music. James Fox would also play some Bob Dylan records as he was a Dylan admirer. Donald Cammell, an acquaintance of the Rolling Stones, as well as a successful artist in his own right, happened to be there as well, reciting poetry from his favourite avant-garde poet: Antonin Artaud. The social event on that occasion later became the subject of a film initiated by Donald Cammell himself, with all of the aspects of that evening conspicuously reflected in the film itself.

And then a few weeks later in the spring of 1968, Donald Cammell started talking about an idea he had in mind: a film about a reclusive rock star and gangster on the lam. The film was centred around Mick Jagger as the main protagonist and was going to be called *Performance*. He was paid $100,000 plus 7.5 per cent of the film's profits.

All the conditions for this project seemed auspicious. Mick Jagger seemed at his best. The directors, Nicholas Roeg and Donald Cammell, were friends of theirs and knew everybody in the film, among them James Fox and Anita Pallenberg. Mick Jagger felt at that time his role as Turner, the jaded rock star, would not be much of a stretch. Everyone would be playing themselves, more or less.

They were making a film of what the public imagined rock stars' lives to be. It was voyeurism that got the financing for the project and has, subsequently, made the film into a cult classic. Warner Brothers envisaged a 'Hollywoodized' version of their inner circle coupled with moral retribution.

The basic situation of the film, Turner and the two women omnipresent in his life, came directly from Donald Cammell's own domestic arrangements in the sixties. Michele Breton plays one of the women in Turner's menage in Paris, where he, Michele Breton and Deborah Dixon, another actress, lived together. Anita Pallenberg, who plays the other woman infatuated with Turner, had only a couple of years earlier had an affair with Donald and Deborah.

Albeit, she also had an affair with Mick Jagger on the set, prompting speculations involving her sex scenes with Mick Jagger for the film. As soon as Keith Richards found out, aside from being hurt, he had just serenaded a song to her 'You Got the Silver', and he subsequently dropped out of performing on the music track for the film, leaving Mick Jagger recording as a solo artist instead.

On another level, the symmetry of the characters in the film mirrored rather too uncannily the relationship between James Fox, Andee Cohen, Marianne Faithfull, and Mick Jagger. Donald Cammell had written the script and woven into it a number of stories, some told to him by Anita Pallenberg and others and the rest from his own experience, so in its own fantastic way, it seemed real.

The story concerned an expanding south London underworld gang emerging from the small time into a big business and a cleaner image. Its boss is Harry Flowers. He has colleagues and a frontman called Chas to do practical work, collect money, threaten lawyers who favoured clients, and destroy rival businesses likely for takeover.

Flowers tell Chas not to do a certain job of destroying a small betting shop belonging to a former friend of Chas, Joey Maddox. Chas disobeys, busts up Joey's shop, and Joey, in revenge, destroys Chas's flat and catches and whips him. Chas, feigning unconsciousness, lunges for a hidden gun to eliminate Joey.

On the run and an embarrassment to Flowers, he hears of a safe place lived in by a recluse rock star, Turner, played by Mick Jagger. He tried to con his way past Turner's mistress, Pherber (Anita Pallenberg), as a juggler. They know he is a criminal on the run but try to help him with a passport photo and medical attention to his back.

Turner also recognises him as an archetypal performer like himself, outside the law, outside society, an assassin. Turner, who has lost his power, his demon, wants to find out Chas' secret and drugs him to try to see inside him. Chas hates dropouts and druggers, and rejects his experiment but spends the night with

Turner's other girlfriend (Michele Breton). The gang find Chas and want to take him away quietly. Turner asks to come too. Chas shoots him.

The film was in two parts: the West End and Chas' domain: and Notting Hill and Turner's flat. For the south London character, James Fox decided to spend a whole week alone in a hotel in Brixton, get a typical haircut and wear nothing but Cecil Gee clothes. Throughout his stay at that hotel in Brixton, he'd be visiting Ronnie Kray, who was dubbed as one of the most dangerous men in London – at that time in Brixton prison – as well as Thomas A Becket pub on Old Kent Road with Johnny Shannon to perfect his accent and manner for his role.

One of the most interesting parts of the film was the London underworld business. The film crew hired real gangsters like Johnny Bindon, who later on got a life sentence for manslaughter, as actors, and a genuine mob boss as an advisor. This was David Litvinoff, who was already part of the 'Swinging Sixties' scene through Robert Fraser and Christopher Gibbs. He was taken on the project as director of authenticity, and all of the gangster dialogue features in the film was under his direction.

The fight scene in Chas' flat was choreographed as a work of art: a recreation of pain, humiliation, love, pride, revenge, weakness, and ruthlessness. But on the other hand, the house in Notting Hill where Mick Jagger's character, Turner, lived in his menage a trois. This is where the talents of Christopher Gibbs were used yet again to create the pop star's private world, arranging a lot of material made and sent from Tangier in a hurry: the bedroom adorned with canopies and furs and soft materials, the bathroom and dressing room in Moroccan mosaics and filled with racks of clothes, the main room stacked with amplifiers and equipment, hung with mirrors, and partitioned with screens.

Part of David Litvinoff's job was to be James Fox's tutor in infamy, immersing James Fox in the netherworld of London. At that point, James Fox had never met anyone like the real-life gangster David Litvinoff; the only gangsters he knew were from central casting. In a sense, most of the cast in *Performance* weren't acting at all, they were simply exhibiting themselves. Real gangsters, real rock stars, real drug addicts, real sirens, everything was real except they were filming what they were doing. By this time, James Fox was almost completely taken by the role. He spoke, thought, and acted like Chas. Donald Cammell cast James Fox as the only professional actor on the set, feeling, as an actor, he could respond according to the director's ideas and suggestions.

With a trained actor there's a separation between what's happening on the set and what you do in your life, but most of the cast of *Performance* were amateurs. One of the first things in acting is how to share the weight, so negative energy is distributed. This protects them while playing a very dark role from being pulled under; James Fox was well aware of this essence of acting as a professional would know all about this, but no one else on the project had a clue.

One's interpretation of Turner was as a symbolic figure. Vaguely tragic, a little pathetic, but still with an edge. He was the archetypal sixties rock apocalypse character, a pre-Raphaelite Hamlet. They carved it out very carefully and put it together, element by element. Behind this characterisation of Turner was the feeling at that time that Mick Jagger's personality was not macabre enough nor damaged enough to support a mythic character such as Turner.

Sadly, it turned out in an occult sort of way to be quite prophetic too. When the project moved to the final shooting script, Mick Jagger became apprehensive. He realised he did not have the faintest idea how to portray his character, given it was his film debut and he was new to acting. He knew, of course, how to act as Mick Jagger in 'real' life, but his character in the film was another thing entirely. The one thing the character could not be was himself.

One of the quirkiest things Donald Cammell did was to switch Mick Jagger's and James Fox's class roles. Mick Jagger played the aristocrat, and James Fox a working-class hood. James Fox became the archetypal servant, while Mick Jagger was the ineffectual blue blood, the very qualities that he always taunted James Fox about throughout their friendship. As a character, Chas was anathema to Turner, and as James Fox got into the part, some of this rubbed off between him and Mick Jagger. Whereas previously, both shared some ironical attitudes, now Mick Jagger in his character became harder, more cynical and a recluse.

Also the film's sexual content reflected the times and the crew's own previous experiences – the idea that one could find gentleness and friendship through sexual intercourse. The conventional identity attitudes that the filmmakers believed were more cultural and inherent within Swinging Sixties society rather than truthful. In other words, *Performance* was truly their *Picture of Dorian Grey*. An allegory of libertine Chelsea life in the late sixties, with its baronial rock stars, drugs, sex, and decadence – it preserves a whole era under glass.

The fusion of life and drama in *Performance* had some aftereffects like a virus infecting everyone. Like song, film is ritual; it precipitates things, gets things going. People who fall through sugar glass skylights often end up falling through real ones, and if ever a film set off a chain reaction, *Performance* was it.

Certainly, Mick Jagger came out of it unaffected; he probably came out of *Performance* with two new characters: the one we already knew of and another, more sinister one: the gangster figure, heart of stone type. If one person came out of a situation like this strong, someone else – no other than James Fox – was the unfortunate one. Although he unequivocally gave the best performance of his acting career, he seemed to have taken a different route in the film. However, James Fox, towards the end of filming, found himself in a slight disagreement with Donald Cammell about the ending.

He, out of curiosity, questioned whether Turner and Pherber really could have believed they'd find the source of the mystery of Chas' personality by dressing him up as an Arabian assassin and feeding him fly agaric mushrooms. He found this a bit naïve, and although he had a great experience on the film set of *Performance,* he found the last few weeks somewhat less enjoyable.

Even James Fox was sympathetic to those ideas in 1968 reflected in the film, although their consequences would cause pain and confusion in his life as well as the lives of his inner circle. The effect the film had on him was to turn him from drugs as a means of self-discovery and spiritual discovery and from the free and uninhibited use of sex as a means of seeking permanent happiness. Cutting himself away from these things, as the film and the part of Chas had already contributed to that, left a void, especially by separating him from the friends whose company he enjoyed. But eventually that was filled by resorting to his childhood religion, the Church of England, getting married and forming a family and taking a break from the film scene for 13 years.

And as for the release of the film, Warner Brothers had qualms about the violencc, sexual content, and whether it was really commercial. The first time the film was shown in Warner Bros studios, an executive famously said, “Even the bath water was dirty.” This referred to a scene depicting Mick Jagger in a bath with Anita Pallenberg and Michele Breton. After going through a great deal of re-editing, censorship, and re-voicing some actors because the studio had feared Americans would find their cockney accents difficult to understand, the film was eventually released two years after the filming was over.

It was soon after *Performance* finished shooting in autumn of 1968 that drug use among their inner circle took a quantum leap. Anita Pallenberg developed a serious heroin habit, and Michele Breton became a drug dealer in Marseille before dying of overdose a few years later. And legend has it that Donald Cammell, the co-director of the film, took his own life a few years later under the same circumstances as in the film, resembling the same pain inflicted by Chas on Turner in the final frames of *Performance*.

IX. IT'S ALL OVER NOW, BABY BLUE

Amid all that haziness, at the beginning of 1968, writer and filmmaker Peter Whitehead embarked on documenting the essence of both the counterculture and anatomy of 'Swinging London' in a film called *Tonite Let's All Make Love in London*. It gave the audience a glimpse into all of the trendiest restaurants, shops, bars, nightclubs, galleries, and casinos in the city and took them through the rudiments of the new English.

Peter Whitehead's disjointed Swinging London is divided into seven 'movements'. The segments are called: Loss of the British Empire, Dollygirls, Protest, It's All Pop Music, Movie Stars, Painting Pop, and followed the last segment called As scene from USA. Each segment depicts a different theme underscored by music. In one of the early segments an early version of Pink Floyd's 'Interstellar Overdrive' could be heard playing behind some arty nightclub scenes, while Chris Farlowe's rendition of the Rolling Stones' 'Out of Time' accompanies a young woman's description of London nightlife and the vacuousness of her own existence.

In another segment, the Marquess of Kensington (Robert Wace) croons the nostalgic 'Changing of the Guard' to shots of Buckingham Palace's changing of the guard, and recording act Vashti are seen at work in the studio between clips of Mick Jagger discussing revolution by the young working-class, whereas Andrew Loog Oldham talks about his future after the Rolling Stones. Julie Christie hugely credits the Beatles for originating the phenomenon known as the Swinging Sixties, while Michael Caine says miniskirts invented by Mary Quant heralded a new era by causing a loss of moral fibre within society.

And finally, novelist Edna O'Brien, describing the promiscuous side of Swinging London, adds, "You meet a boy now, or a man, and you don't really have to protest about your virginity. In fact, it will be a great disappointment to him if you say, you know, it's the first time, I mean he'll leave the room."

However, Peter Whitehead was adamant by making the film that counterculture in Britain did not start with miniskirts and pop music but with the Aldermaston march, Vanessa Redgrave, and the Bertrand Russell Peace Foundation as a vehement opponent of US imperialism and the Vietnam war. *Tonite Let's Make Love in London* was also about the warfare going on in the United States, with the bombing of Vietnam resulting in violent anti-war demonstrations across Europe. But most significant of all is Chris Farlowe's rendition of the Rolling Stones song written and produced for him by them: 'Out of Time'. Signalling perhaps that the counterculture revolution initiated in London may now be reaching the end of the spectrum, and it was all coming to a bitter end.

The startling thing about the making and the release of it in 1968, was it coincided exactly with a period of violent protests sweeping throughout western Europe: 10,000 Sorbonne students rioted in Paris, 5,000 anti-war protesters charged a thousand policemen in front of the American embassy in Grosvenor Square in London and in August 1968, an estimated 300 demonstrators were injured in charges against the national guard in Chicago. A decade which had started with all the old certainties in place, during which fashion, music and art, and films too had changed their style. Fantasy had usurped social realism, and a violent surge of creative energy in Britain in the sixties had drawn European and American filmmakers, each with their own particular views on London; all ended in an attempted revolution.

Recreational drugs were also synonymous with Swinging Sixties London and became more commonly used in the latter part of the decade. Marijuana, cannabis, and LSD were in circulation and flowing free among British pop stars. It was very difficult for anyone in show business to avoid becoming involved in drugs in some way and easily influenced young people looking for fun were encouraged to follow their idols and take hallucinogenic drugs. There were even rumours circulating that the Beatles' big single 'Lucy in the Sky with Diamonds', which featured on their highly successful album *Sgt. Pepper's Lonely Heart Club Band,* was code for LSD. The effects of these drugs were also reflected in psychedelic art and films, bringing new, vibrant, and exciting colours and patterns to the forefront.

The *Yellow Submarine* film, with its combination of psychedelic pictures and music, illustrates this perfectly. Marianne Faithfull, Mick Jagger, Keith Richards, Donovan, Robert Fraser, John Lennon, George Harrison, and Pattie Boyd all had charges against them for possession of either marijuana, cannabis, or LSD. The death of Brian Jones due to a drug overdose jeopardised the legacy of the Swinging Sixties, resulting in trivial and unfair interpretations of all the changes that the young teenagers at the time strove to bring about. However, ironically, the police officer who between 1967 and '68 launched a 'witch hunt' to get all the British pop idols in Britain arrested for possession of drugs and in some cases planting drugs to make it easier to press charges against them, Sergeant Pilcher, was himself arrested for embezzlement at the beginning of the following decade, spending four years in prison.

The British film mood of the sixties began with Barrett in *The Servant* waging silent class warfare against his master, and it ended with an East End gangster losing his mind in the colour-saturated flat in Notting Hill. London had become the city that everyone wanted to hang out in; it had the music, the fashion, and many young things, and for a while, everything shot better over there. In the sixties, there was a real attempt by disreputable young filmmakers to break away from the stiff-upper-lip school of British films. As they struggled to come to terms with the rapidly changing society, they produced some ground-breaking films, but some unfortunately memorable failures too. However, what was really significant about that era was the feeling of confidence and vitality that it generated in the industry, allowing the directors to have the films they wanted to make in Britain and Hollywood come over to make them. However, it has become fashionable now to overlook the sixties, to undervalue the fundamental changes that took place in that decade, and to dismiss the cinema of that period without even knowing it. But, retrospectively, should we not be prouder of that decade of films, which were moving, stylish, and experimental, and struck chords with millions of cinema-goers. What are we doing now to rival what was going on then?

In the sixties, a band from Northern Ireland – Them – recorded a cover of a Bob Dylan song 'It's All Over Now, Baby Blue'. By now, the end of Swinging Sixties London was looming; it captured the mood of a bygone era, a decade which defined and empowered youth for many generations to come.

CATALOGUE OF SWINGING SIXTIES FILMS

1. A Hard Day's Night (1964)
2. The Knack ...and How to Get It (1965)
3. Darling (1965)
4. The Pleasure Girls (1965)
5. The Party's Over (1965)
6. Blow-Up (1966)
7. Alfie (1966)
8. Morgan: A Suitable Case for Treatment (1966)
9. Here We Go Round the Mulberry Bush (1968)
10. Joanna (1968)
11. Performance (1970)
12. Bedazzled (1967)
13. Smashing Time (1967)
14. Deep End (1970)
15. Privilege (1967)
16. Georgy Girl (1966)

17. I'll Never Forget What's'isname (1967)
18. The Magic Christian (1969)
19. Up the Junction (1968)
20. Catch Us If You Can (1965)
21. Tonite Let's All Make Love in London (1967)
22. Ferry Cross the Mersey (1964)
23. Pop Gear (1965)
24. Help! (1965)
25. Poor Cow (1967)
26. To Sir, with Love (1967)
27. UK Swings Again (1964)
28. Pop Gear (1965)
29. Swinging U.K. (1964)
30. Wonderful Life (1964)
31. Wonderwall (1968)
32. Play It Cool (1962)
33. The Big T.N.T. Show (1966)
34. The System (1964)
35. Magic Christian (1969)
36. Yellow Submarine (1968)
37. The Rolling Stone Rock and Roll Circus (1968)
38. The Jokers (1967)
39. Modesty Blaise (1966)

40. The L-Shaped Room (1962)
41. Be My Guest (1965)
42. Live it Up! (1963)
43. Dateline Diamonds (1965)
44. When the Boys Meet the girls (1966)
45. Hold on! (1966)
46. Mrs. Brown, You've Got a Lovely Daughter (1968)
47. Rotten to the Core (1965)
48. Press for Time (1966)
49. The Guru (1969)
50. Comedy Man (1964)

A SWINGING SIXTIES KING'S ROAD MAP

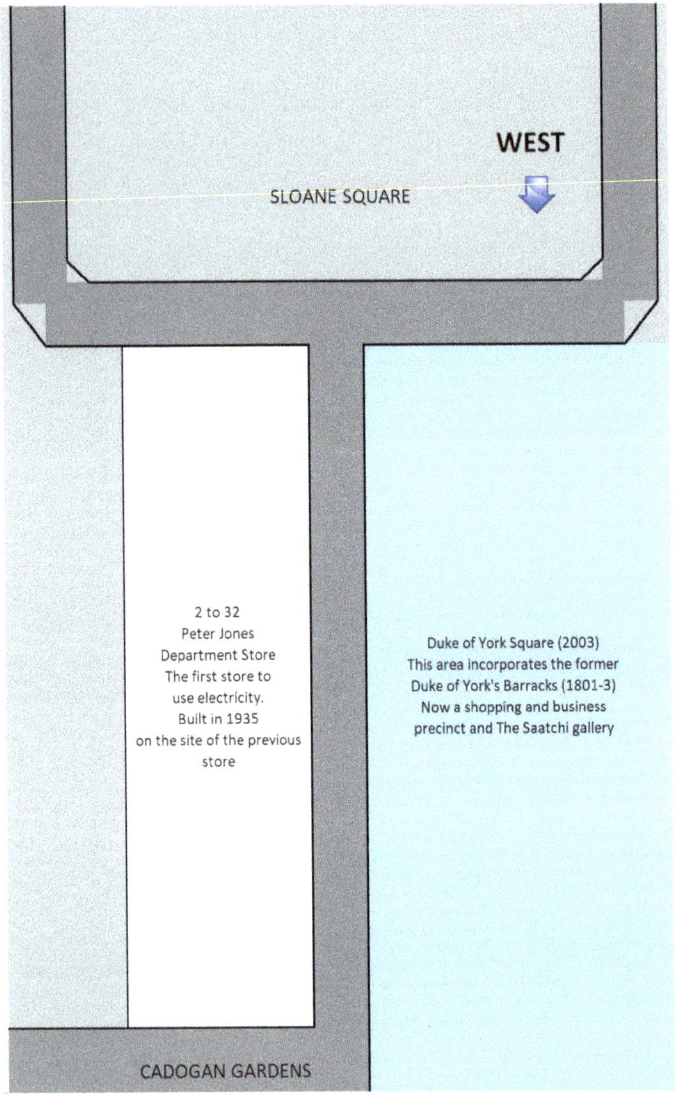
WEST
SLOANE SQUARE
2 to 32
Peter Jones
Department Store
The first store to
use electricity.
Built in 1935
on the site of the previous
store
Duke of York Square (2003)
This area incorporates the former
Duke of York's Barracks (1801-3)
Now a shopping and business
precinct and The Saatchi gallery
CADOGAN GARDENS

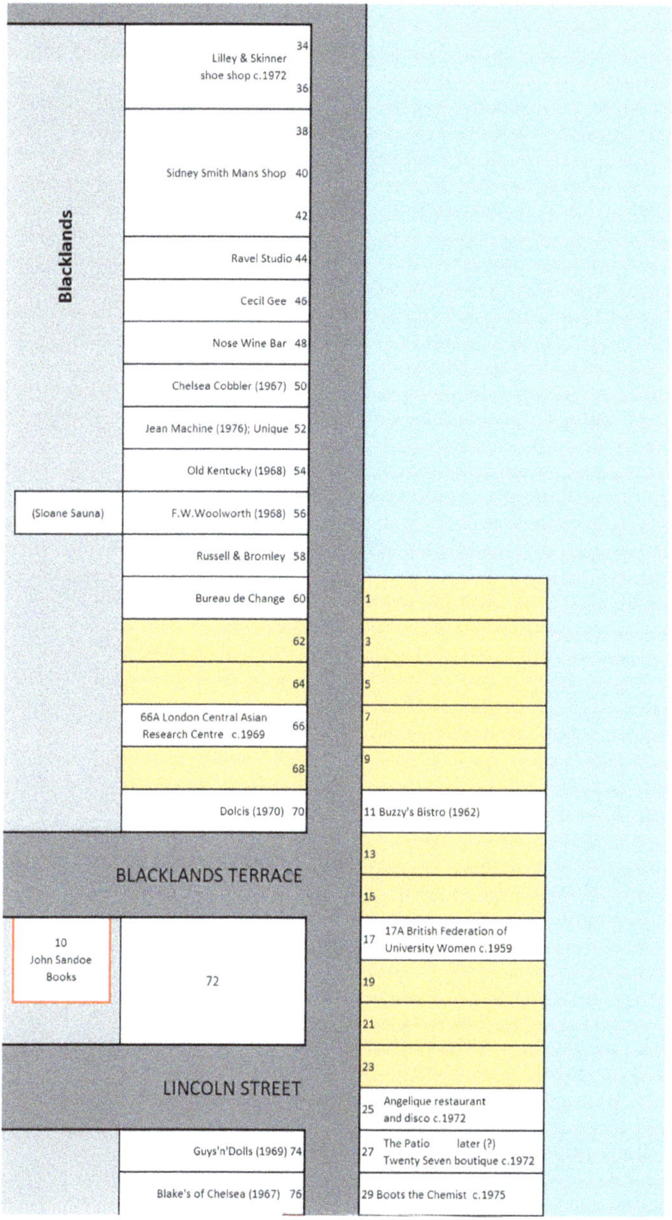
Blacklands
34
Lilley & Skinner
shoe shop c.1972
36
38
Sidney Smith Mans Shop 40
42
Ravel Studio 44
Cecil Gee 46
Nose Wine Bar 48
Chelsea Cobbler (1967) 50
Jean Machine (1976); Unique 52
Old Kentucky (1968) 54
(Sloane Sauna)
F.W.Woolworth (1968) 56
Russell & Bromley 58
Bureau de Change 60
62
64
66A London Central Asian
Research Centre c.1969
66
68
Dolcis (1970) 70
BLACKLANDS TERRACE
10
John Sandoe
Books
72
LINCOLN STREET
Guys'n'Dolls (1969) 74
Blake's of Chelsea (1967) 76
1
3
5
7
9
11 Buzzy's Bistro (1962)
13
15
17
17A British Federation of
University Women c.1959
19
21
23
25
Angelique restaurant
and disco c.1972
27
The Patio later (?)
Twenty Seven boutique c.1972
29 Boots the Chemist c.1975

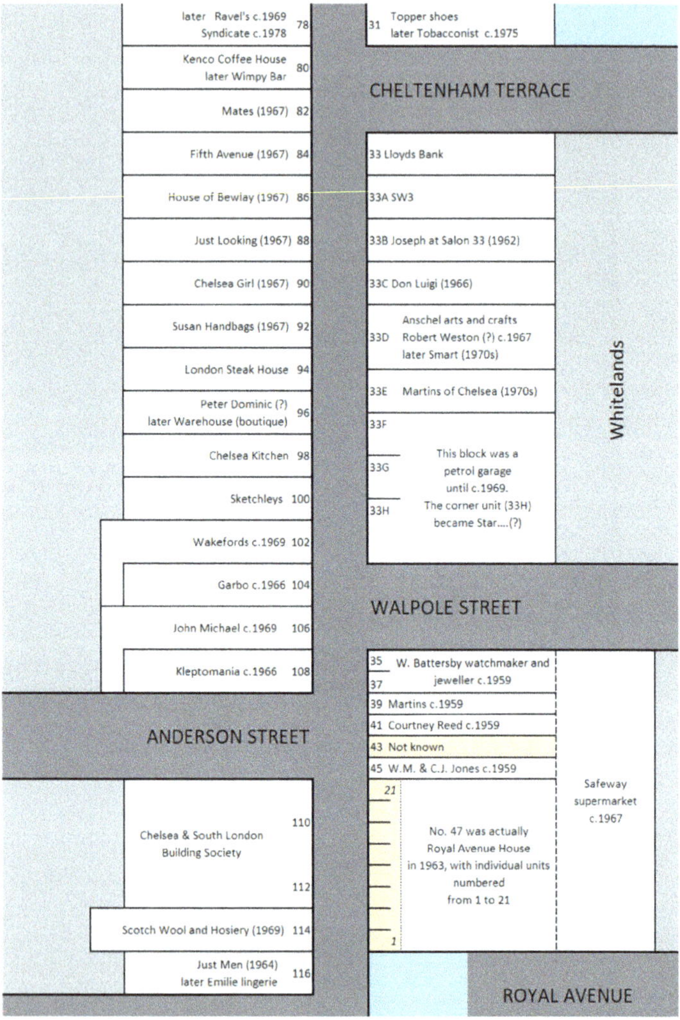
later Ravel's c.1969 Syndicate c.1978 78
Kenco Coffee House later Wimpy Bar 80
Mates (1967) 82
Fifth Avenue (1967) 84
House of Bewlay (1967) 86
Just Looking (1967) 88
Chelsea Girl (1967) 90
Susan Handbags (1967) 92
London Steak House 94
Peter Dominic (?) later Warehouse (boutique) 96
Chelsea Kitchen 98
Sketchleys 100
Wakefords c.1969 102
Garbo c.1966 104
John Michael c.1969 106
Kleptomania c.1966 108
ANDERSON STREET
110 Chelsea & South London Building Society 112
Scotch Wool and Hosiery (1969) 114
Just Men (1964) later Emilie lingerie 116
31 Topper shoes later Tobacconist c.1975
CHELTENHAM TERRACE
33 Lloyds Bank
33A SW3
33B Joseph at Salon 33 (1962)
33C Don Luigi (1966)
33D Anschel arts and crafts Robert Weston (?) c.1967 later Smart (1970s)
33E Martins of Chelsea (1970s)
33F
33G
33H
This block was a petrol garage until c.1969. The corner unit (33H) became Star....(?)
Whitelands
WALPOLE STREET
35 37 W. Battersby watchmaker and jeweller c.1959
39 Martins c.1959
41 Courtney Reed c.1959
43 Not known
45 W.M. & C.J. Jones c.1959
21
1
No. 47 was actually Royal Avenue House in 1963, with individual units numbered from 1 to 21
Safeway supermarket c.1967
ROYAL AVENUE

A SWINGING SIXTIES KING'S ROAD MAP

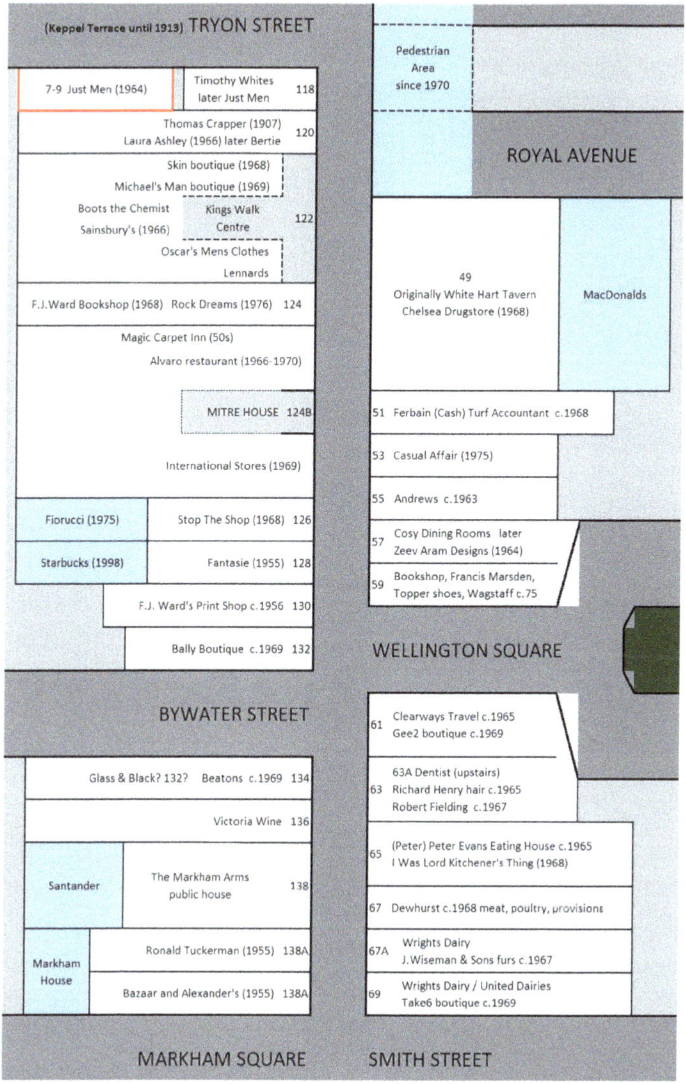

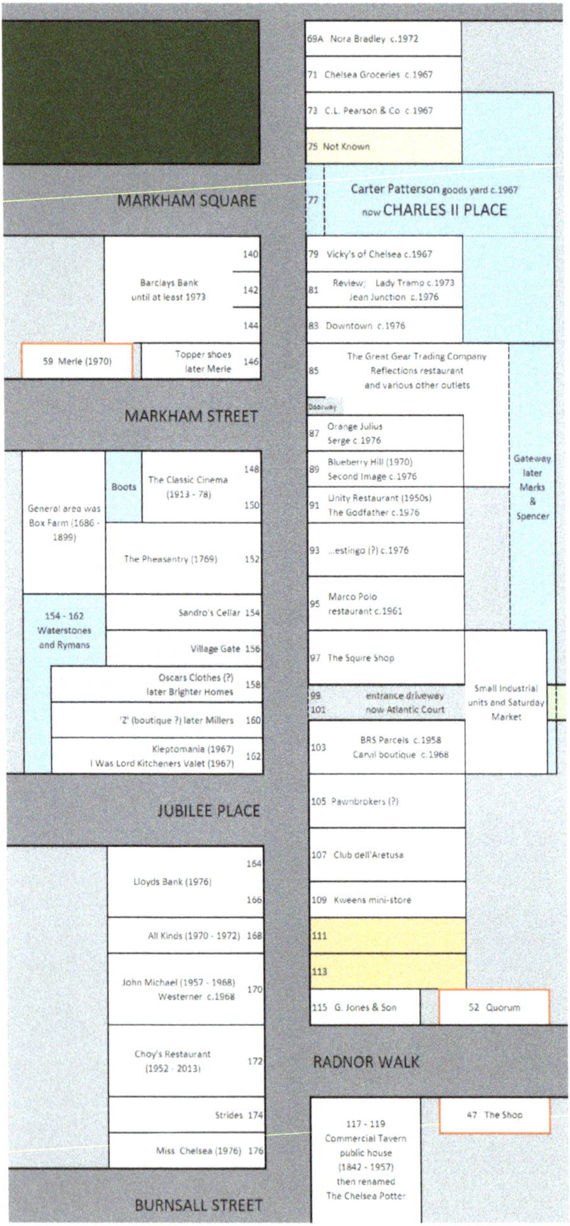
69A Nora Bradley c.1972
71 Chelsea Groceries c.1967
73 C.L. Pearson & Co c.1967
75 Not Known
MARKHAM SQUARE
77
Carter Patterson goods yard c.1967
now CHARLES II PLACE
140
Barclays Bank
until at least 1973
142
144
79 Vicky's of Chelsea c.1967
81 Review; Lady Tramp c.1973
Jean Junction c.1976
83 Downtown c.1976
59 Merle (1970)
Topper shoes
later Merle
146
85 The Great Gear Trading Company
Reflections restaurant
and various other outlets
MARKHAM STREET
Doorway
87 Orange Julius
Serge c.1976
General area was
Box Farm (1686 - 1899)
Boots
The Classic Cinema
(1913 - 78)
148
150
89 Blueberry Hill (1970)
Second Image c.1976
91 Unity Restaurant (1950s)
The Godfather c.1976
Gateway
later
Marks
&
Spencer
The Pheasantry (1769) 152
93 ...estingo (?) c.1976
154 - 162
Waterstones
and Rymans
Sandro's Cellar 154
Village Gate 156
95 Marco Polo
restaurant c.1961
97 The Squire Shop
Oscars Clothes (?)
later Brighter Homes
158
'Z' (boutique ?) later Millers 160
Kleptomania (1967)
I Was Lord Kitcheners Valet (1967)
162
99
101
entrance driveway
now Atlantic Court
Small Industrial
units and Saturday
Market
103 BRS Parcels c.1958
Carvil boutique c.1968
JUBILEE PLACE
105 Pawnbrokers (?)
164
Lloyds Bank (1976)
166
107 Club dell'Aretusa
109 Kweens mini-store
All Kinds (1970 - 1972) 168
111
113
John Michael (1957 - 1968)
Westerner c.1968
170
115 G. Jones & Son
52 Quorum
Choy's Restaurant
(1952 - 2013)
172
RADNOR WALK
Strides 174
Miss Chelsea (1976) 176
117 - 119
Commercial Tavern
public house
(1842 - 1957)
then renamed
The Chelsea Potter
47 The Shop
BURNSALL STREET

A SWINGING SIXTIES KING'S ROAD MAP

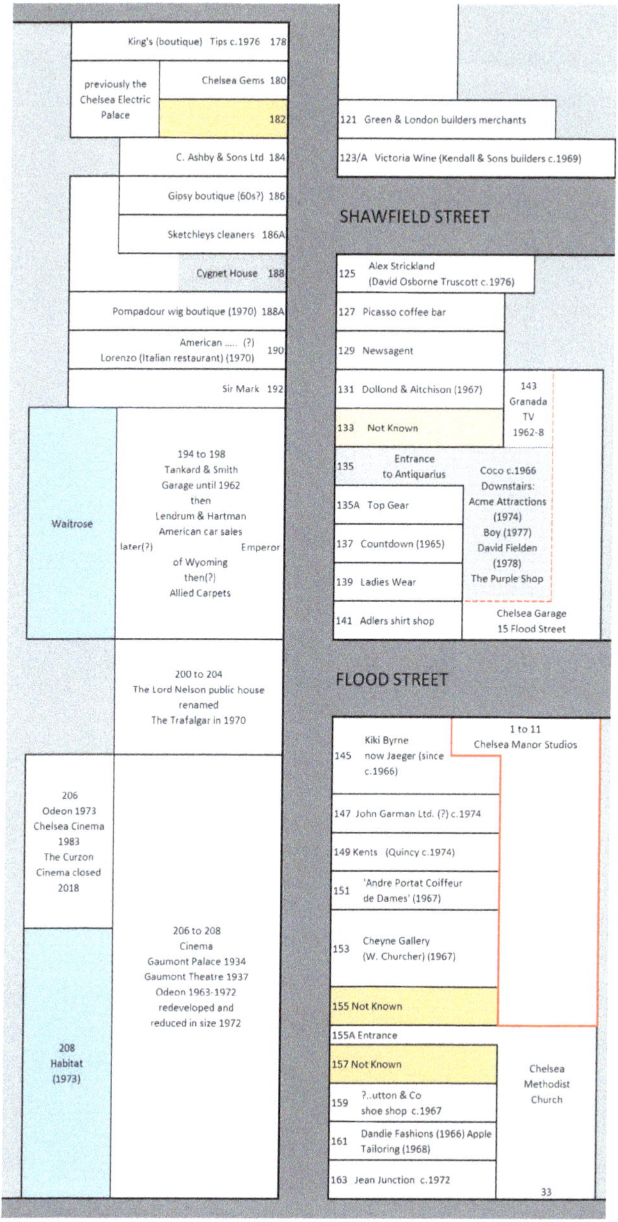

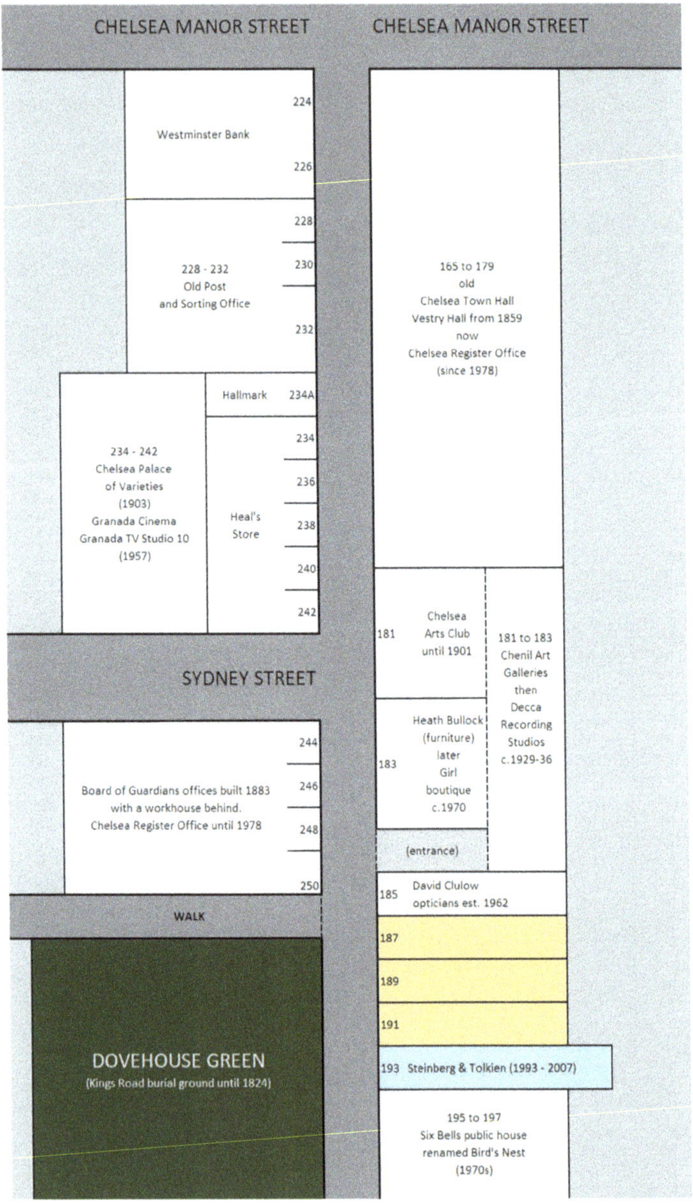
CHELSEA MANOR STREET
CHELSEA MANOR STREET
224
Westminster Bank
226
228
230
228 - 232
Old Post
and Sorting Office
232
165 to 179
old
Chelsea Town Hall
Vestry Hall from 1859
now
Chelsea Register Office
(since 1978)
Hallmark
234A
234
236
234 - 242
Chelsea Palace
of Varieties
(1903)
Granada Cinema
Granada TV Studio 10
(1957)
Heal's
Store
238
240
242
181
Chelsea
Arts Club
until 1901
181 to 183
Chenil Art
Galleries
then
Decca
Recording
Studios
c.1929-36
SYDNEY STREET
183
Heath Bullock
(furniture)
later
Girl
boutique
c.1970
244
246
Board of Guardians offices built 1883
with a workhouse behind.
Chelsea Register Office until 1978
248
(entrance)
250
185
David Clulow
opticians est. 1962
WALK
187
189
191
DOVEHOUSE GREEN
(Kings Road burial ground until 1824)
193 Steinberg & Tolkien (1993 - 2007)
195 to 197
Six Bells public house
renamed Bird's Nest
(1970s)

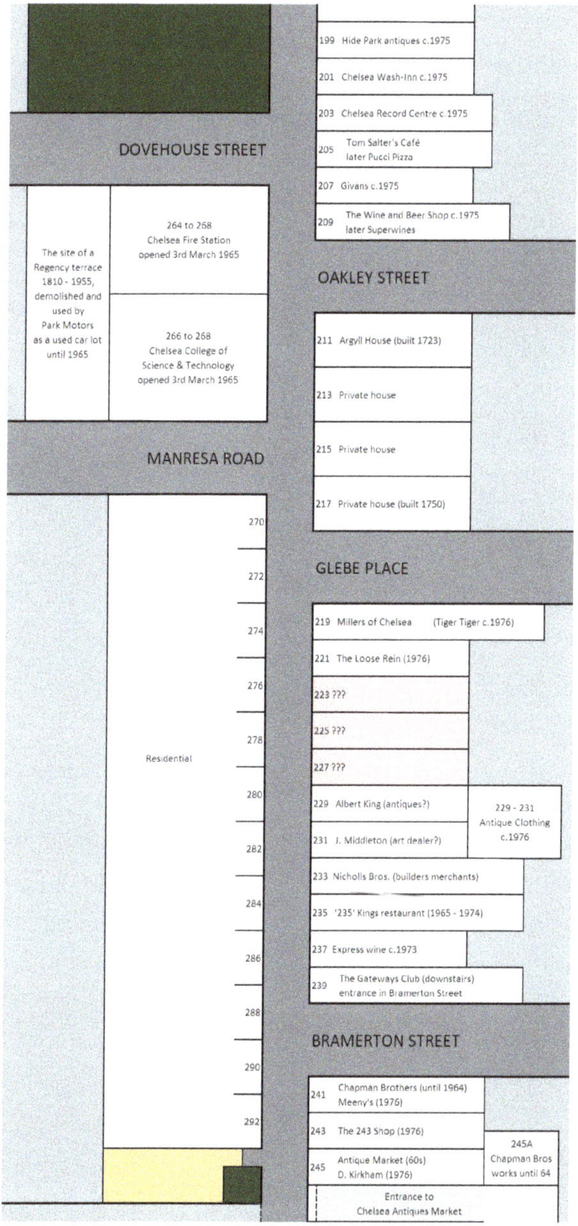
DOVEHOUSE STREET
The site of a Regency terrace 1810 - 1955, demolished and used by Park Motors as a used car lot until 1965
264 to 268 Chelsea Fire Station opened 3rd March 1965
266 to 268 Chelsea College of Science & Technology opened 3rd March 1965
MANRESA ROAD
Residential
270
272
274
276
278
280
282
284
286
288
290
292
199 Hide Park antiques c.1975
201 Chelsea Wash-Inn c.1975
203 Chelsea Record Centre c.1975
205 Tom Salter's Café later Pucci Pizza
207 Givans c.1975
209 The Wine and Beer Shop c.1975 later Superwines
OAKLEY STREET
211 Argyll House (built 1723)
213 Private house
215 Private house
217 Private house (built 1750)
GLEBE PLACE
219 Millers of Chelsea (Tiger Tiger c.1976)
221 The Loose Rein (1976)
223 ???
225 ???
227 ???
229 Albert King (antiques?)
231 J. Middleton (art dealer?)
229 - 231 Antique Clothing c.1976
233 Nicholls Bros. (builders merchants)
235 '235' Kings restaurant (1965 - 1974)
237 Express wine c.1973
239 The Gateways Club (downstairs) entrance in Bramerton Street
BRAMERTON STREET
241 Chapman Brothers (until 1964) Meeny's (1976)
243 The 243 Shop (1976)
245 Antique Market (60s) D. Kirkham (1976)
245A Chapman Bros works until 64
Entrance to Chelsea Antiques Market

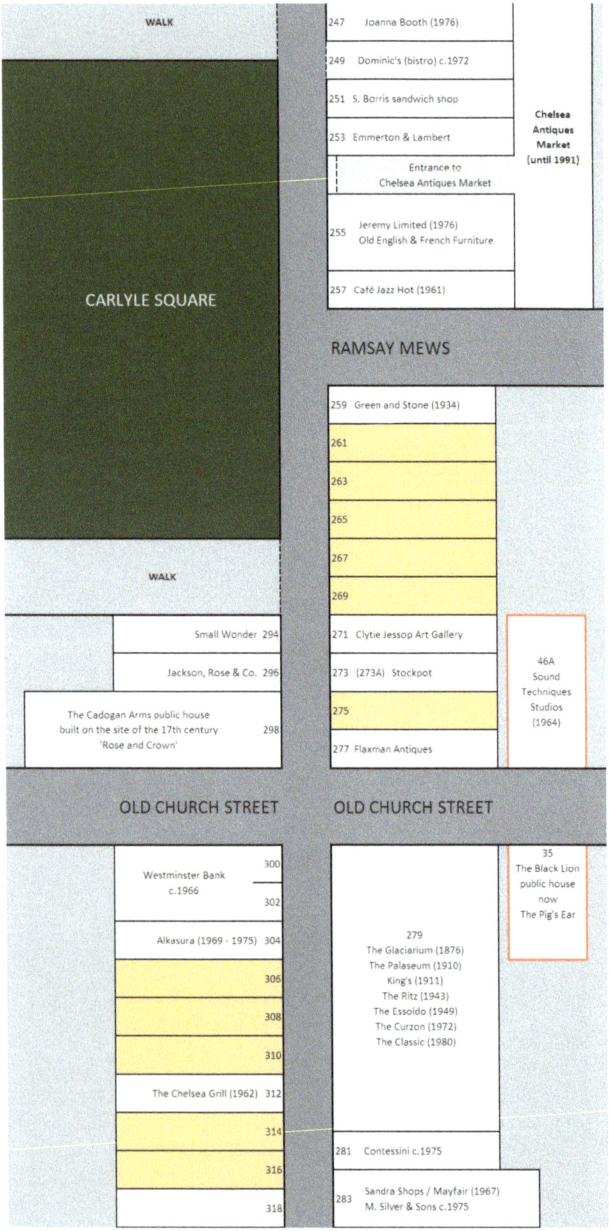
WALK
247 Joanna Booth (1976)
249 Dominic's (bistro) c.1972
251 S. Borris sandwich shop
253 Emmerton & Lambert
Entrance to Chelsea Antiques Market
Chelsea Antiques Market (until 1991)
255 Jeremy Limited (1976) Old English & French Furniture
257 Café Jazz Hot (1961)
CARLYLE SQUARE
RAMSAY MEWS
259 Green and Stone (1934)
261
263
265
267
269
WALK
271 Clytie Jessop Art Gallery
273 (273A) Stockpot
275
277 Flaxman Antiques
Small Wonder 294
Jackson, Rose & Co. 296
The Cadogan Arms public house built on the site of the 17th century 'Rose and Crown' 298
46A Sound Techniques Studios (1964)
OLD CHURCH STREET
OLD CHURCH STREET
Westminster Bank c.1966 300 302
Alkasura (1969 - 1975) 304
306
308
310
The Chelsea Grill (1962) 312
314
316
318
35 The Black Lion public house now The Pig's Ear
279 The Glaciarium (1876) The Palaseum (1910) King's (1911) The Ritz (1943) The Essoldo (1949) The Curzon (1972) The Classic (1980)
281 Contessini c.1975
283 Sandra Shops / Mayfair (1967) M. Silver & Sons c.1975

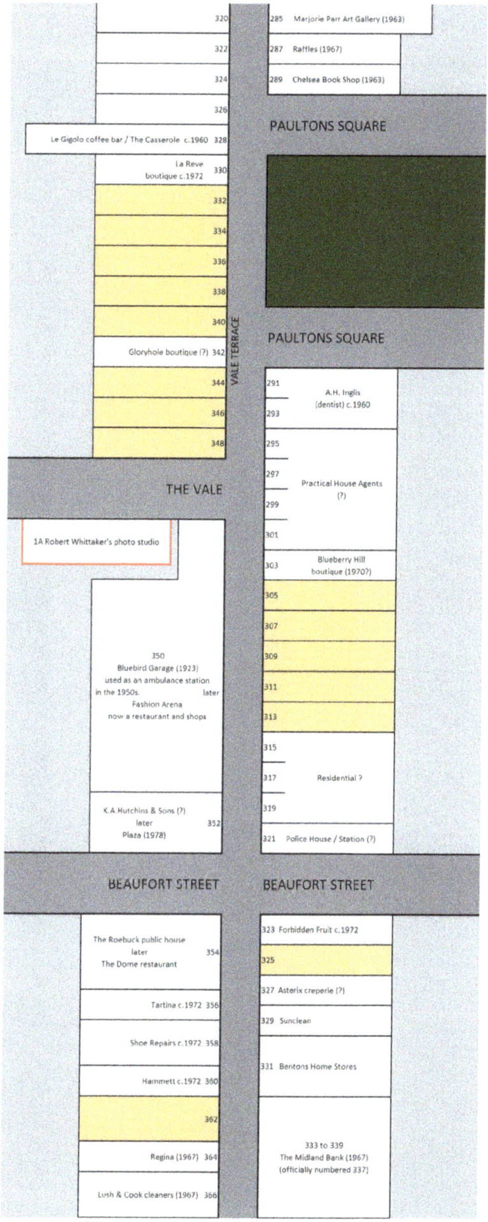
320
285 Marjorie Parr Art Gallery (1963)
322
287 Raffles (1967)
324
289 Chelsea Book Shop (1963)
326
PAULTONS SQUARE
Le Gigolo coffee bar / The Casserole c.1960 328
La Reve boutique c.1972 330
332
334
336
338
340
PAULTONS SQUARE
Gloryhole boutique (?) 342
VALE TERRACE
344
346
348
291
A.H. Inglis (dentist) c.1960
293
295
297
Practical House Agents (?)
299
301
THE VALE
1A Robert Whittaker's photo studio
303 Blueberry Hill boutique (1970?)
305
307
309
311
313
350
Bluebird Garage (1923)
used as an ambulance station
in the 1950s. later
Fashion Arena
now a restaurant and shops
315
317 Residential ?
319
K.A.Hutchins & Sons (?) later Plaza (1978) 352
321 Police House / Station (?)
BEAUFORT STREET
BEAUFORT STREET
The Roebuck public house later The Dome restaurant 354
323 Forbidden Fruit c.1972
325
327 Asterix creperie (?)
Tartina c.1972 356
329 Sunclean
Shoe Repairs c.1972 358
331 Bentons Home Stores
Hammett c.1972 360
362
333 to 339
The Midland Bank (1967)
(officially numbered 337)
Regina (1967) 364
Lush & Cook cleaners (1967) 366

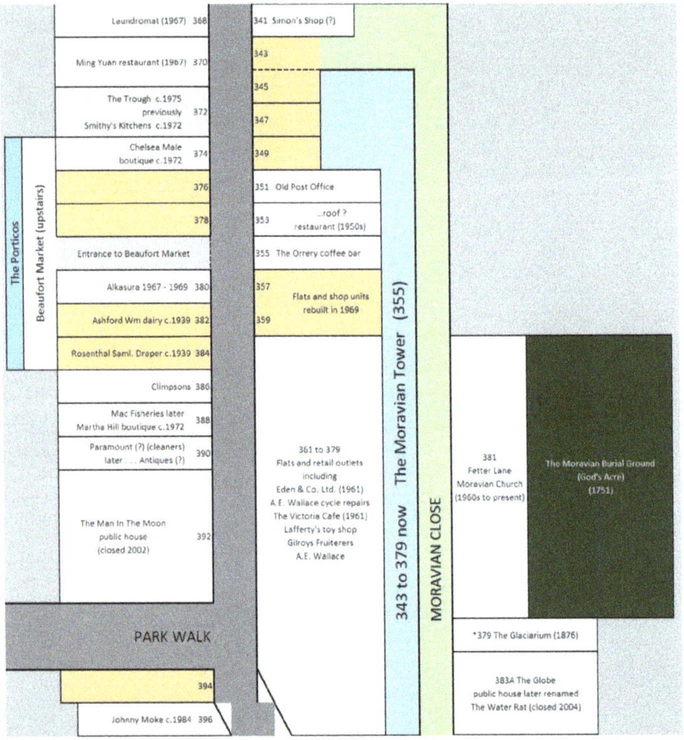
Laundromat (1967) 368
Ming Yuan restaurant (1967) 370
The Trough c.1975 previously Smithy's Kitchens c.1972 372
Chelsea Male boutique c.1972 374
376
378
Entrance to Beaufort Market
Alkasura 1967 - 1969 380
Ashford Wm dairy c.1939 382
Rosenthal Saml. Draper c.1939 384
Climpsons 386
Mac Fisheries later Martha Hill boutique c.1972 388
Paramount (?) (cleaners) later . . . Antiques (?) 390
The Man In The Moon public house (closed 2002) 392
The Porticos
Beaufort Market (upstairs)
PARK WALK
394
Johnny Moke c.1984 396
341 Simon's Shop (?)
343
345
347
349
351 Old Post Office
353 ...roof ? restaurant (1950s)
355 The Orrery coffee bar
357
359
Flats and shop units rebuilt in 1969
361 to 379
Flats and retail outlets including
Eden & Co. Ltd. (1961)
A.E. Wallace cycle repairs
The Victoria Cafe (1961)
Lafferty's toy shop
Gilroys Fruiterers
A.E. Wallace
343 to 379 now The Moravian Tower (355)
MORAVIAN CLOSE
381 Fetter Lane Moravian Church (1960s to present)
The Moravian Burial Ground (God's Acre) (1751)
*379 The Glaciarium (1876)
383A The Globe public house later renamed The Water Rat (closed 2004)

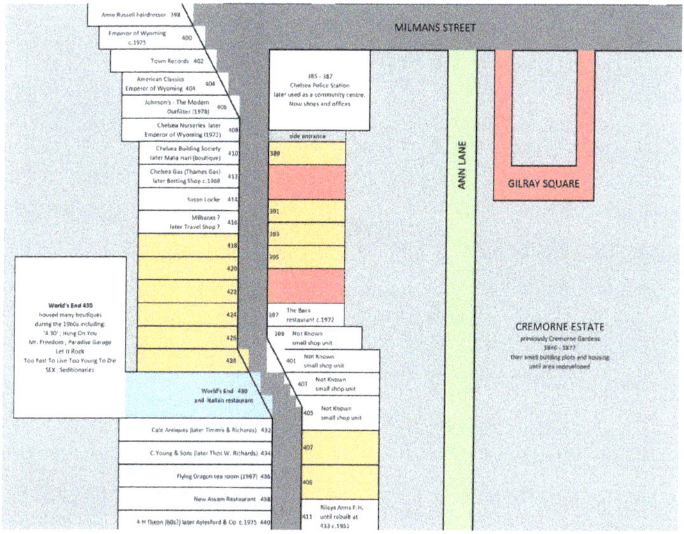
MILMANS STREET
Anne Russell hairdresser 398
Emperor of Wyoming c.1975 400
Town Records 402
American Classics Emperor of Wyoming 404 404
Johnson's - The Modern Outfitter (1978) 406
Chelsea Nurseries later Emperor of Wyoming (1972) 408
Chelsea Building Society later Mata Hari (boutique) 410
Chelsea Gas (Thames Gas) later Betting Shop c.1960 412
Susan Locke 414
Milbanks ? later Travel Shop ? 416
418
420
422
424
426
428
World's End 430
housed many boutiques
during the 1960s including:
'430' ; Hung On You
Mr. Freedom ; Paradise Garage
Let It Rock
Too Fast To Live Too Young To Die
SEX ; Seditionaries
World's End 430 and Italian restaurant
Cale Antiques (later Timmis & Richards) 432
C.Young & Sons (later Thos W. Richards) 434
Flying Dragon tea room (1967) 436
New Assam Restaurant 438
A H Dixon (60s?) later Aylesford & Co c.1975 440
385 - 387
Chelsea Police Station
later used as a community centre.
Now shops and offices
side entrance
389
391
393
395
397 The Barn restaurant c.1972
399 Not Known small shop unit
401 Not Known small shop unit
403 Not Known small shop unit
405 Not Known small shop unit
407
409
411 Rileys Arms P.H. until rebuilt at 433 c.1952
ANN LANE
GILRAY SQUARE
CREMORNE ESTATE
previously Cremorne Gardens

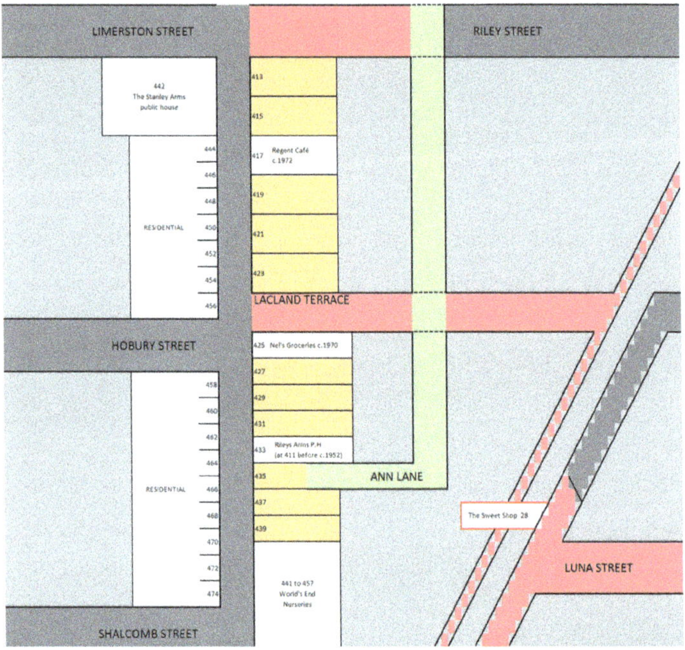
LIMERSTON STREET
RILEY STREET
442
The Stanley Arms
public house
RESIDENTIAL
444
446
448
450
452
454
456
413
415
417
Regent Café
c.1972
419
421
423
LACLAND TERRACE
HOBURY STREET
425 Nel's Groceries c.1970
427
429
431
433
Rileys Arms P.H
(at 411 before c.1952)
435
437
439
ANN LANE
RESIDENTIAL
458
460
462
464
466
468
470
472
474
441 to 457
World's End
Nurseries
The Sweet Shop 28
LUNA STREET
SHALCOMB STREET

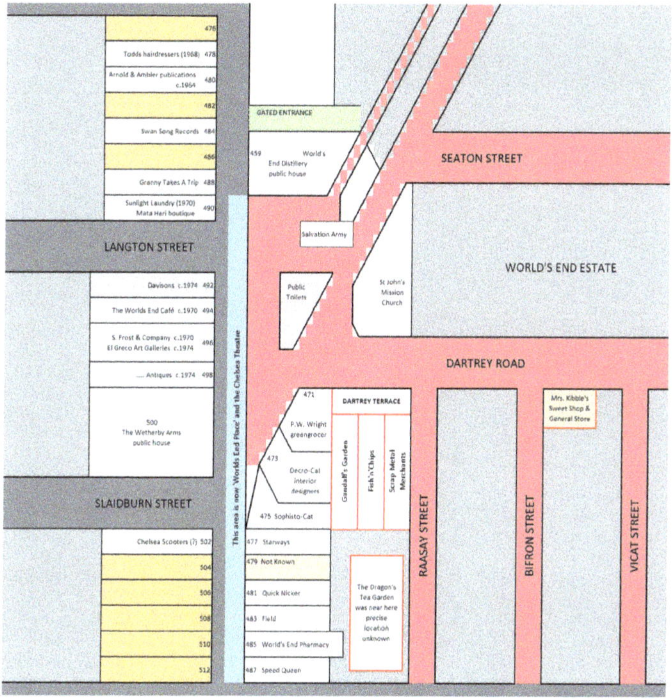
476
Todds hairdressers (1968) 478
Arnold & Ambler publications c.1964 480
482
Swan Song Records 484
486
Granny Takes A Trip 488
Sunlight Laundry (1970) Mata Hari boutique 490
LANGTON STREET
Davisons c.1974 492
The Worlds End Café c.1970 494
S. Frost & Company c.1970 El Greco Art Galleries c.1974 496
.... Antiques c.1974 498
500 The Wetherby Arms public house
SLAIDBURN STREET
Chelsea Scooters (?) 502
504
506
508
510
512
This area is now 'Worlds End Place' and the Chelsea Theatre
GATED ENTRANCE
459 World's End Distillery public house
Salvation Army
Public Toilets
St John's Mission Church
SEATON STREET
WORLD'S END ESTATE
DARTREY ROAD
471
P.W. Wright greengrocer
473
Decro-Cat interior designers
475 Sophisto-Cat
477 Starways
479 Not Known
481 Quick Nicker
483 Field
485 World's End Pharmacy
487 Speed Queen
DARTREY TERRACE
Gandalf's Garden
Fish'n'Chips
Scrap Metal Merchants
The Dragon's Tea Garden was near here precise location unknown
RAASAY STREET
Mrs. Kibble's Sweet Shop & General Store
BIFRON STREET
VICAT STREET

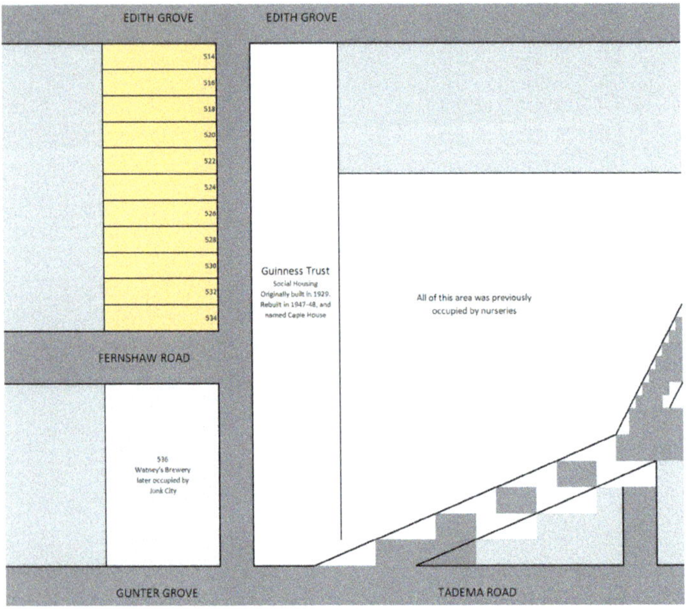
EDITH GROVE
EDITH GROVE
514
516
518
520
522
524
526
528
530
532
534
Guinness Trust
Social Housing
Originally built in 1929.
Rebuilt in 1947-48, and
named Caple House
All of this area was previously
occupied by nurseries
FERNSHAW ROAD
536
Watney's Brewery
later occupied by
Junk City
GUNTER GROVE
TADEMA ROAD

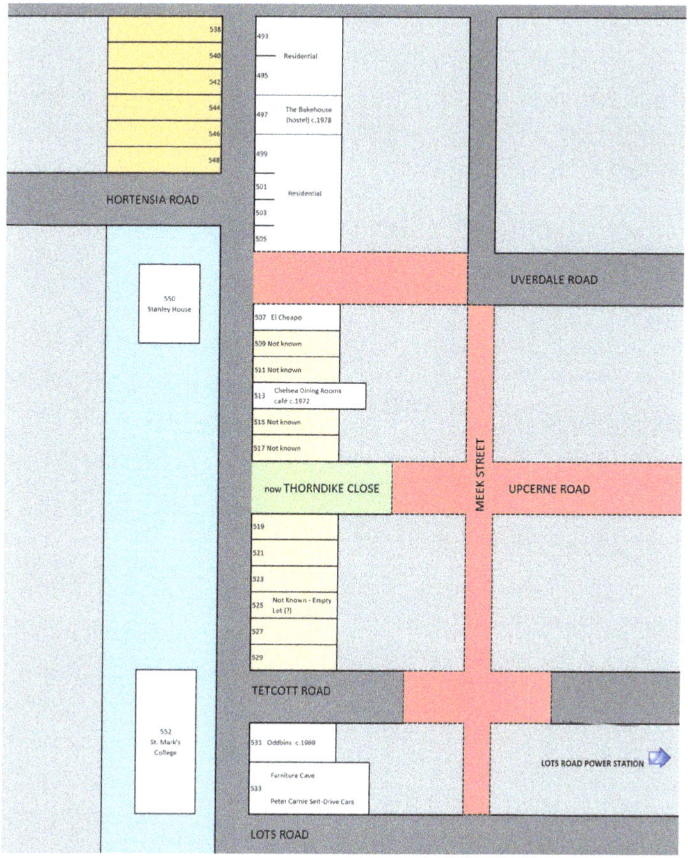
538
540
542
544
546
548
493
Residential
495
497
The Bakehouse (hostel) c.1978
499
501
Residential
503
505
HORTENSIA ROAD
UVERDALE ROAD
550
Stanley House
507 El Cheapo
509 Not known
511 Not known
513
Chelsea Dining Rooms café c.1972
515 Not known
517 Not known
now THORNDIKE CLOSE
MEEK STREET
UPCERNE ROAD
519
521
523
525
Not Known - Empty Lot (?)
527
529
TETCOTT ROAD
552
St. Mark's College
531 Oddbins c.1969
Furniture Cave
533
Peter Carnie Self-Drive Cars
LOTS ROAD POWER STATION
LOTS ROAD

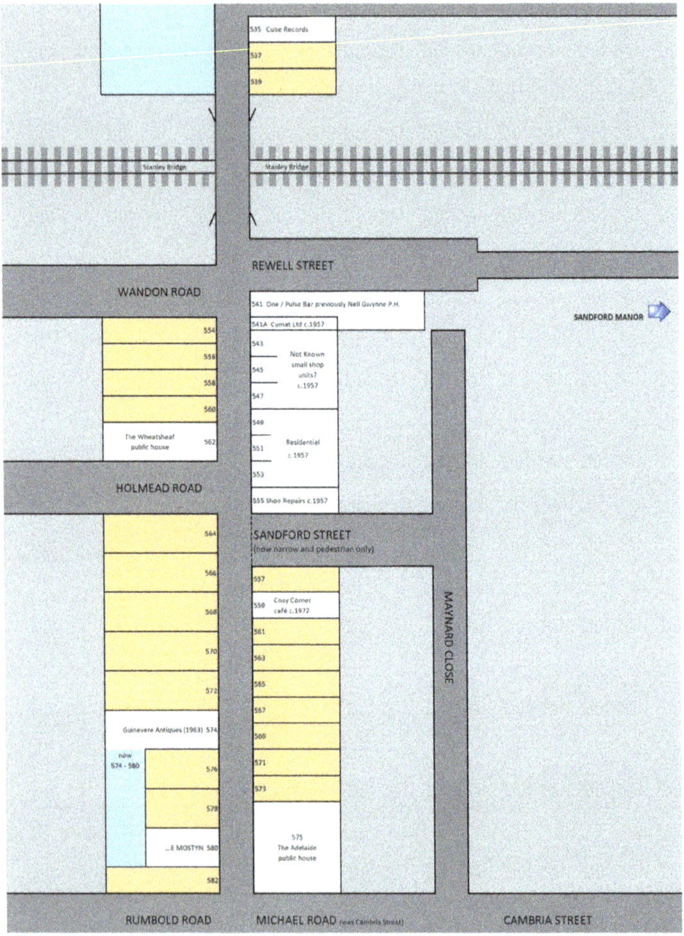

535 Cube Records
537
539
Stanley Bridge
Stanley Bridge
REWELL STREET
WANDON ROAD
541 One / Pulse Bar previously Nell Gwynne P.H.
541A Cumat Ltd c.1957
SANDFORD MANOR
543
545
547
Not Known small shop units? c.1957
549
551
553
Residential c.1957
555 Shoe Repairs c.1957
554
556
558
560
The Wheatsheaf public house 562
HOLMEAD ROAD
SANDFORD STREET
(now narrow and pedestrian only)
564
566
568
570
572
Guinevere Antiques (1963) 574
now 574 - 580
576
578
...E MOSTYN 580
582
557
559 Cosy Corner café c.1972
561
563
565
567
569
571
573
575 The Adelaide public house
MAYNARD CLOSE
RUMBOLD ROAD
MICHAEL ROAD (was Cambria Street)
CAMBRIA STREET

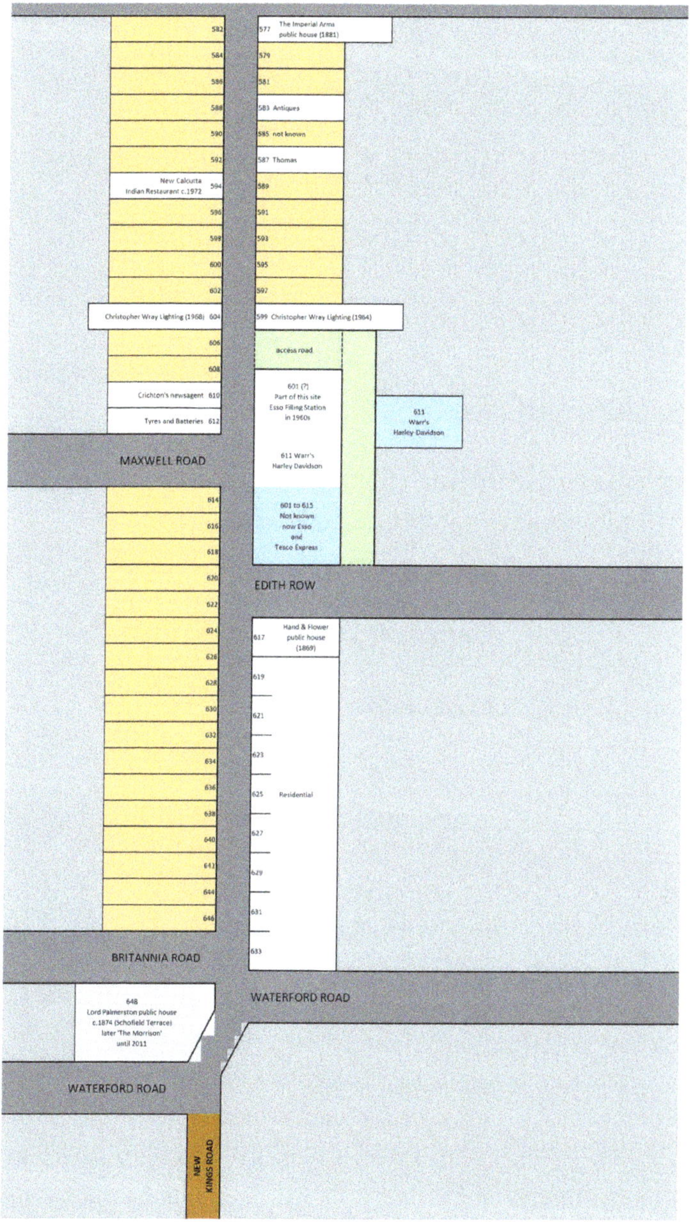
582
584
586
588
590
592
New Calcutta Indian Restaurant c.1972 594
596
598
600
602
Christopher Wray Lighting (1968) 604
606
608
Crichton's newsagent 610
Tyres and Batteries 612
MAXWELL ROAD
614
616
618
620
622
624
626
628
630
632
634
636
638
640
644
646
BRITANNIA ROAD
648 Lord Palmerston public house c.1874 (Schofield Terrace) later 'The Morrison' until 2011
WATERFORD ROAD
NEW KINGS ROAD
577 The Imperial Arms public house (1881)
579
581
583 Antiques
585 not known
587 Thomas
589
591
593
595
597
599 Christopher Wray Lighting (1964)
access road
601 (?) Part of this site Esso Filling Station in 1960s
611 Warr's Harley Davidson
601 to 615 Not known now Esso and Tesco Express
611 Warr's Harley Davidson
EDITH ROW
617 Hand & Flower public house (1869)
619
621
623
625 Residential
627
629
631
633
WATERFORD ROAD

PICTURE ACKNOWLEDGEMENTS

1. Author's father during the swinging sixties (Courtesy of author)

2. Author's father at the Rolling Stones free concert - Altamont in 1969 (Courtesy of author)

3. Lee Harris playing alongside Orson Welles (Courtesy of Amira & Lee Harris)

4. Mods in Soho, London, 1963 (Courtesy of Amira & Lee Harris)

5. Swinging Sixties model Amanda Lear (Courtesy of Amanda Lear)

6. London 1967 with Amanda Lear (Courtesy of Amanda Lear)

7. A sketch titled 'Their New Incarnation' of the Beatles (Courtesy of Gerald Scarfe)

8. The Rolling Stones at 102 Edith Grove in Chelsea (Courtesy of Florian & Frank Habicht) .

9. Plastic Ono Band Xmas 1969 London (Courtesy of Amira & Lee Harris)

10. A portrait of photographer David Bailey (Courtesy of Author)

11. Author chatting with legendary Sir Michael Caine (Courtesy of Author)

12. Julie Christie, a Swinging Sixties icon (Courtesy of Author)

13. Author chatting with Elton John (Courtesy of Author)

14. Author interviewing actor Terrence Stamp (Courtesy of Author)

15. Author interviewing actor James Fox (Courtesy of Author)

16. Author interviewing the late photographer Terry O'Neill (Courtesy of Author)

SELECT BIBLIOGRAPHY

Ann-Jones, Leslie. *Ride A White Swan: The Lives and Death of Marc Bolan* (Hodder & Stroughton, 2012)

Beaton, Cecil. *Parting Years: Diaries, 1963-74* (Littlehampton Book Services, 1978)

Clapton, Eric. *The Autobiography* (Century,2007)

Collins, Joan. *Past Imperfect* (Simon & Schuster,1984)

Cooper, Michael. *Michael Cooper: The London Sixties* (Schirmer/Mosel,1999)

Connolly, Ray. *In The Sixties* (Pavilion, 1995)

Des Barres, Pamela. *I am With The Band: Confession of A Groupie* (Beech Tree Books,1987)

Diski, Jenny. *The Sixties* (Profile Books, 2010)

Faithfull, Marianne. *Memories, Dreams and Reflections* (Harper Perennial, 2008)

Feeney Callan, Michael. *Julie Christie* (W.H. Allen/ Virgin Books, 1984)

Fletcher, Tony. *Dear Boy: The Life of Keith Moon* (Omnibus Press, 2005)

Garner, Phillip; Alan Mellor, David. *Antonioni's Blow-Up* (Steidel, 2011)

Gilbert, Lewis. *All My Flashbacks: The Autobiography of Lewis Gilbert Sixty Years a Film Director* (Reynolds & Hearn, 2010)

Harrison, George. *I, Me, Mine* (Genesis Publications, 1980)

Hemmings, David. Blow-Up and other Exaggerations (Robson Books, 2004)

Hewitt, Paolo. *Steve Marriott: All Too Beautiful: It's All So Beautiful -The Life and Times of Steve Marriott* (Helter Skelter Publishing, 2004)

Isherwood, Christopher. *The Sixties: Diaries Volume Two 1960-1969* (Chatto & Windus, 2010)

Johns, Glyn. *Sound Man: A Life Recording Hits with The Rolling Stones, The Who, Led Zepplin, The Eagles, Eric Clapton, The Faces...* (Blue Rider Press, 2014)

Lawson, Leslie. *Twiggy: An Autobiography* (Hart-Davis MacGibbon, 1975)

Lear, Amanda. *My Life with Dali* (Virgin Books, 1985)

Liechfield, Patrick. *Not The Whole Truth* (Constable, 1986)

Miles, Barry. *In The Sixties.* (Jonathan Cape, 2002)

Miles, Sarah. *A Right Royal Bastard* (Phoenix, 1996)

Miles, Sarah. *Serves Me Right* (Macmillan, 1994)

Norman, Philip. *Mick Jagger* (Ecco Press, 2012)

O'Brian, Lucy. *Dusty: Biography of Dusty* Springfield (Sidgwick & Jackson, 1999)

O'Dell, Chris. Miss O'Dell: Hard Days and Long Nights with The Beatles, The Stones, Bob Dylan and Eric Clapton (Touchstone, 2009)

Loog Oldham, Andrew. *Stoned* (Vintage, 2001)

Pim, Keiron. *Jumpin' Jack Flash: David Litvinoff and the Rock'n'Roll Underworld* (Vintage, 2017)

Quant, Mary. *Quant by Quant.* (C. Chivers, 1974)

Reed, Jeremy. *The King of Carnaby Street: A Life of John Stephen* (Haus Publishing, 2010)

Richards. Keith. *Life* (Back Bay Books, 2011)

Sandbrook, Dominic. *White Heat: A History of Britain in the Swinging Sixties* (Abacus, 2007)

Sassoon, Vidal. *Vidal: The Autobiography* (Macmillan, 2010)

Savage, Jon. *1966:The Year the Decade Exploded* (Faber & Faber, 2016)

Schell, Catherine. *A Constant Alien* (Fantom Films Limited, 2016)

Seller, Robert. *What Fresh Lunacy is This?: The Authorized Biography of Oliver Reed* (Constable & Robinson, 2014)

Shrimpton, Jean. *Jean Shrimpton: An Autobiography* (Ebury Press, 1990)

Sinclair, Andrew. *A View of the Sixties* (Sinclair Stevenson,1994)

Stamp, Terrence. *Coming Attractions* (Bloomsbury Publishing, 1989)

Stamp, Terrence. *Double Feature* (Bloomsbury Publishing, 1989)

Stone, Paulene. *One Tear is Enough* (Michael Joseph, 1975)

Street-Porter, Janet. *Fall Out: A Memoir of Friends Made and Friends Unmade* (Headline Review, 2006)

Taylor, Derek. *As Time Goes By: Living in the Sixties with John Lennon, Paul McCartney, George Harrison, Ringo Starr, Brian Epstein, Allen Klein, Mae West, Brian ... Los Angeles, New York City, and on the Road* (Faber & Faber, 2018)

Townshend, Pete. *Pete Townshend: Who I Am* (Harper Collins, 2013)

Trynka, Paul. *Brian Jones: The Making of a Rolling Stone* (Plume, 2015)

Tynan, Kenneth. *The Diaries of Kenneth Tynan* (Bloomsbury Publishing, 2002)

Vickers, Hugo. *Beaton in the Sixties: The Cecil Beaton Diaries As He Wrote Them, 1965-1969* (Alfred A Knopf, 2004)

Vyner, Harriet. *Groovy Bob: The Life and Times of Robert Fraser* (Faber and Faber, 2001)

Winner, Michael. *Michael Winner: Winner Takes All: A Life of Sorts* (Robson Books, 2013)

Other Sources

www.sixtiescity.net/Culture/KingsRoad2.htm

www. flashbak.com/blow-up-swinging-sixties-stockwell-9386/

www.thehistorypress.co.uk/articles/the-swinging-sixties/

Other Materials

British Invasion: Herman's Hermits Documentary

British Cinema In The 60s BBC Documentary

The Real Blow Up Sixties Film Documentary

Cecil Beaton by David Bailey Documentary

Brian Duffy: The Man Who Shot the Sixties

Twiggy Documentary by Biography Channel

Bob Dylan: Don't Look Back Documentary

My Generation: The Small Faces Documentary

The Beatles: Anthology Series Documentary

Eric Clapton: Life in 12 Bars Documentary

Bill Wyman: The Quiet One Documentary

Ronnie Wood: Somebody Up There Likes Me

The Stones In The Park Documentary

My Generation Documentary

My Life As A Rolling Stone

Quant Documentary

FURTHER READING

King, Tony. *The Tastemaker: My Life with the Legends and Geniuses of Rock Music* (Faber & Faber, 2023)

Phillipe, Norman. *We Danced On Our Desks: Brilliance and backstabbing at the Sixties' most influential magazine* (Mensch Publishing, 2022)

Boyd, Pattie. *My Life In Pictures* (Reel Art Press, 2022)

Blackwell, Chris. *The Islander: My Life in Music and Beyond* (Nine Eight Books, 2022)

Davies, Dave. *Living On A Thin Line* (Headline, 2022)

Sexton, Paul. *Charlie's Good Tonight: The Authorised Biography of The Rolling Stones' Charlie Watts* (Mudlark, 2022)

Higgs, John. *Love and Let Die: Bond, the Beatles and the British Psyche* (W&N, 2022)

Jones, Ann-Leslie. *The Stone Age: Sixty Years of the Rolling Stones* (John Blake 2022)

Dylan, Bob. *The Philosophy Of Modern Music* (Simon & Schulster, 2022)

McCartney, Paul. *The Lyrics:1956 to the Present* (Allen Lane, 2021)

Kennington, Jill. *Model Years* (Unicorn, 2021)

Mills, Hayley. *Forever Young: A Memoir* (W&N, 2021)

Otter Bickerdike, Jennifer. *You Are Beautiful and You Are Alone: The Biography of Nico* (Faber & Faber 2021)

Hepworth, David. *Abbey Road: The Inside Story of the World's Most Famous Recording Studio* (Bantam Press, 2021)

H Wells, Simon. *She's a Rainbow: The Extraordinary Life of Anita Pallenberg* (Omnibus Press, 2020)

Sheff, David. *All We Are Saying: The Last Major Interview with John Lennon and Yoko Ono* (Pan, 2020)

Boyd, Jenny. *Jennifer Juniper: A journey beyond the muse* (Urbane, 2020)

Brown, Craig. *One Two Three Four: The Beatles in Time: Winner of the Baillie Gifford Prize* (Fourth Estate, 2020)

Neil, Andy. *Ready, Steady, Go! The Weekend Starts Here: The Definitive Story of the Show That Changed Pop TV* (BMG Books, 2020)

Bailey, David. *Look Again* (Macmillan, 2020)

Raj, Bent. *The Rolling Stones In the Beginning* (Mitchell Beazley, 2020)

Mulrennan, Kevin. *Thank Your Lucky Stars: The 60's Pop Show Featuring The Kinks, The Beatles And The Rolling Stones* (Independently Published, 2020)

Myers, Laurence. *Hunky Dory (Who Knew?): The best I can remember from twenty years at the heart of '60s and '70s rock and* pop (B&B Books, 2019)

Wells, Simon. *London Life: The Magazine of the Swinging Sixt*ies (Omnibus Press, 2020)

Lister, Jenny. *Mary Quant* (V&A, 2019)

Hulanicki, Barbara. *From A to Biba The Autobiography of Barbara Hulanicki* (V&A, 2019)

Caine, Michael. *Blowing the Bloody Doors Off: And Other Lessons in Life* (Hodder Paperbacks, 2019)

Checksfield, Peter. *Top Of The Pops: The Years Rediscovered 1964-1975* (Independently Published, 2019)

Wyman, Bill. *Stones From The Inside: Rare and Unseen Images* (ACC Art Books, 2019)

Star, Ringo. *Another Day In The Life: My Life in Music and photos* (Genesis Publications, 2019)

Ann-Jones, Leslie. *Ride A White Swan: The Lives and Death of Marc Bolan* (Hodder & Stroughton, 2012)

Beaton, Cecil. *Parting Years: Diaries, 1963-74* (Littlehampton Book Services, 1978)

Clapton, Eric. *The Autobiography (Century, 2007)*

Connolly, Ray. *In The Sixties* (Pavilion, 1995)

Des Barres, Pamela. *I am With The Band: Confession of A Groupie* (Beech Tree Books, 1987)

Diski, Jenny. *The Sixties* (Profile Books, 2010)

Faithfull, Marianne. *Memories, Dreams and Reflections* (Harper Perennial, 2008)

Feeney Callan, Michael. *Julie Christie* (W.H. Allen/Virgin Books, 1984)

Fletcher, Tony. *Dear Boy: The Life of Keith Moon* (Omnibus Press, 2005)

DAILY EXPRESS

TUESDAY MARCH 26 1963

Missing model speaks

I was bewildered she says

CHRISTINE—AT LAST

After 17 days of silence she tells of her travels

RODNEY HALLWORTH and FRANK HOWITT

CHRISTINE KEELER swung her high-booted legs over a swish chair in a Madrid flat tonight and said: "Suddenly I feel a load has been lifted from my mind."

The missing model had spent the night less comfortably, perched on two straight-backed chairs in a back-street police station.

quote

Suddenly I feel a load has been lifted from my mind. In the next few days I will decide when I will go home.

'HELP'

CORRECT

NEXT MOVE

TRIP

HUSH! UNIONS ARE ANGRY AT BEECHING CUT-DOWN

Napoleon's bed flies in

Davey Moore dies—'neck hit rope'

Squirrel attacks housewife

'Zoo' man fined

Resort closes as doctors accuse

Naps up!

and The Scout leads in a winner

A Premier retires after 20 years

RADIO and TV

FLEet-street 8000

Victim

France faces power cuts

The bomb hunt in the woods

Sports car PC injured

POCKET CARTOON

Raid on tomb

Ex-coach is found shot at Harrow

Father gives boy kidney

The dog they left behind

Arias on bail

JUST FANCY THAT

Why TRU GEL gives your hair the groomed but casual look

TRU GEL

LOOK FOR THIS LIVELY NEW PACK

Daily Mirror

3d. Thursday, June 6, 1963 No. 18,494

WAR MINISTER SCANDAL

"I have come to realise that, by this deception, I have been guilty of a grave misdemeanour"

PROFUMO QUITS

He lied to MPs over Christine to save his family

Mirror Comment

THE BIG LIE

THE Daily Mirror does not kick a man when he is down.

Mr. Profumo, who married a beautiful and pleasant woman, is now down and out.

There can be nothing but pity for a suave but tarnished politician who has to admit—in a letter to his Prime Minister—that he is guilty of lying, of misleading, of deception, and of a grave misdemeanour. The words of the confession were chosen by Profumo himself.

God knows, he was never a good Minister; it seems now that he is not a very important man. But there is guilt in many a human heart, and skeletons in many cupboards.

The question is:

What the hell is going on in this country?

Morals

All power corrupts—and the Tories have been in power for nearly twelve years. They are certainly enduring their full quota of fallen idols, whited sepulchres, and off-white morals.

In the Commons, Mr. Profumo made a personal statement in March,

BEFORE THE STORM

Smiling happily, before the storm broke . . . Mr. John Profumo pictured with his beautiful wife, former actress Valerie Hobson. Now he is a Minister no longer. And his political career is in ruins.

By VICTOR KNIGHT

WAR MINISTER JOHN PROFUMO caused a political sensation last night by resigning from the Government.

In a dramatic letter to the Prime Minister Mr Profumo admitted that he lied to the Commons about his association with red-haired model Christine Keeler "to protect my wife and family."

This admission finally clears away the cloud of rumour and suspicion which has hung over the political scene for more than three months.

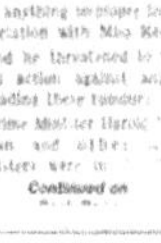

Christine Keeler

The first public hint of a scandal building up around 48-year-old Mr. Profumo came during a Commons debate in the early hours of March 22.

Three Labour MPs referred to rumours surrounding 21-year-old Miss Keeler who was then a missing witness in an Old Bailey shooting case.

A few hours later Mr. Profumo made a personal [illegible]

[illegible] was anything improper in his association with Miss Keeler.

And he threatened to take legal action against anyone spreading these rumours.

Prime Minister Harold Macmillan and other senior Ministers were in [illegible]

Continued on [illegible]

Rolling Stones Captures Top Spot in Teen Charts

Teen Beat...

21—Rome News-Tribune February 26, 1967

By JEANNE HARRISON
Columbia Features, Inc.

The Rolling Stones were rolling uphill in both the single and album race. Their hit single, "Ruby Tuesday," took over the top position while their album, "Between The Buttons" displaced "Sound of Music" in the number five album spot.

Making a move for the top were The Supremes with "Love Is Here To Stay and Now You've Gone" going from fifth to third in the singe department.

TOP TEN SINGLES

"Ruby Tuesday" — The Rolling Stones

"Georgy Girl" — The Seekers

"Love Is Here And Now You're Gone — The Supremes

"Kind Of A Drag" — The Buckinghams

"I'm A Believer" — The Monkees

"Gimme Some Loving" — Spencer Davis Group

"We Ain't Got Nothing' Yet" — The Blue Magoos

"The Beat Goes On" — Sonny and Cher

"Then You Can Tell Me Goodbye" — The Casinos

"Green, Green Of Home" — Tom Jones

TOP FIVE ALBUMS

"More Of The Monkees" — The Monkees

"The Monkees — The Monkees

"S.R.O." — Tijuana Brass

"Dr. Zhivago" — Sound Track

"Between The Buttons" — The Rolling Stones

The first new single in a long time for the Beatles is "Strawberry Fields Forever." A fine, unusual ballad. Other new singles worth the spinning are: "Dedicated To The One I Love," The Mamas and The Papas; "Return Of The Red Baron," The Royal Guardsmen; "Yellow Balloon," Jan and Dean; and "Words," The Nashville Teens.

Sonny and Cher's latest album, "In Case You're In Love," is a winner as is "Georgy Girl," by The Seekers.

Pepperell, Model Represented . . . .

Floyd Band Students Participate in Meet

By MARTHA PARKER
Teen Beat Correspondent

Last Saturday morning — February 18, in fact — at the unearthly hour of 6:30 a.m., a bus containing eight sleepy Pepperell band members arrived at Model to pick up eight equally sleepy Model band members. These sixteen people were just beginning a very long day as representatives of their schools at the 7th District Band Clinic at Rossville.

Each year schools from all over the 7th district send some of their band students to the clinic. This year over 300 students from more than 20 schools made up three all-district bands. During the morning, all band members auditioned for chair placement in their pre-assigned band. The three bands, Red, White, and Blue practiced part of the morning and all Saturday afternoon under the direction of top directors. Each band gave a concert at the Rossville Community Center Saturday night.

At the concert, the people who were first chair first in their sections were awarded certificates of merit. Teresa Lee and Steve Dodd of Model received these certificates in their sections.

Students attending were Cheryl Atkins, Charles Barnett, Johnny Dudley, Sidney Farrar, Jan Gilbert, Sue Mull, Diane Oswald, and Lisa Taylor. These students were accompanied by Bobby Henderson and Don Leithauser, Model and Pepperell band directors, respectively.

Area School Roundup

MODEL

Mike Mathis, Penny Jones, and Johnette Tate were elected as president, vice president and secretary of the junior class.

Represenative of the University of Georgia presented a program to the 10th through 12th grades Tuesday.

"Youth Wants to Know" programs were presented to the freshman class Tuesday and to the senior girls Thursday.

FBLA members are beginning projects for the state convention in April.

The Model Senior Tri-Hi-Y won the Club of the Month

PRINTING HOUSE SQUARE, LONDON, E.C.4. TELEPHONE: 01-236 2000

WHO BREAKS A BUTTERFLY ON A WHEEL?

MR. JAGGER has been sentenced to imprisonment for three months. He is appealing against conviction and sentence, and has been granted bail until the hearing of the appeal later in the year. In the meantime, the sentence of imprisonment is bound to be widely discussed by the public. And the circumstances are sufficiently unusual to warrant such discussion in the public interest.

MR. JAGGER was charged with being in possession of four tablets containing amphetamine sulphate and methyl amphetamine hydrochloride; these tablets had been bought, perfectly legally, in Italy, and brought back to this country. They are not a highly dangerous drug, or in proper dosage a dangerous drug at all. They are of the benzedrine type and the Italian manufacturers recommend them both as a stimulant and as a remedy for travel sickness.

In Britain it is an offence to possess these drugs without a doctor's prescription. MR. JAGGER'S doctor says that he knew and had authorized their use, but he did not give a prescription for them as indeed they had already been purchased. His evidence was not challenged. This was therefore an offence of a technical character, which before this case drew the point to public attention any honest man might have been liable to commit. If after his visit to the POPE the ARCHBISHOP of CANTERBURY had bought proprietary airsickness pills on Rome airport, and imported the unused tablets into Britain on his return, he would have risked committing precisely the same offence. No one who has ever travelled and bought proprietary drugs abroad can be sure that he has not broken the law.

JUDGE BLOCK directed the jury that the approval of a doctor was not a defence in law to the charge of possessing drugs without a prescription, and the jury convicted. MR. JAGGER was not charged with complicity in any other drug offence that occurred in the same house. They were separate cases, and no evidence was produced to suggest that he knew that MR. FRASER had heroin tablets or that the vanishing MR. SNEIDERMANN had cannabis resin. It is indeed no offence to be in the same building or the same company as people possessing or even using drugs, nor could it reasonably be made an offence. The drugs which MR. JAGGER had in his possession must therefore be treated on their own, as a separate issue from the other drugs that other people may have had in their possession at the same time. It may be difficult for lay opinion to make this distinction clearly, but obviously justice cannot be done if one man is to be punished for a purely contingent association with someone else's offence.

We have, therefore, a conviction against MR. JAGGER purely on the ground that he possessed four Italian pep pills, quite legally bought but not legally imported without a prescription. Four is not a large number. This is not the quantity which a pusher of drugs would have on him, nor even the quantity one would expect in an addict. In any case MR. JAGGER'S career is obviously one that does involve great personal strain and exhaustion; his doctor says that he approved the occasional use of these drugs, and it seems likely that similar drugs would have been prescribed if there was a need for them. Millions of similar drugs are prescribed in Britain every year, and for a variety of conditions.

One has to ask, therefore, how it is that this technical offence, divorced as it must be from other people's offences, was thought to deserve the penalty of imprisonment. In the courts at large it is most uncommon for imprisonment to be imposed on first offenders where the drugs are not major drugs of addiction and there is no question of drug traffic. The normal penalty is probation, and the purpose of probation is to encourage the offender to develop his career and to avoid the drug risks in the future. It is surprising therefore that JUDGE BLOCK should have decided to sentence MR. JAGGER to imprisonment, and particularly surprising as MR. JAGGER'S is about as mild a drug case as can ever have been brought before the Courts.

It would be wrong to speculate on the JUDGE'S reasons, which we do not know. It is, however, possible to consider the public reaction. There are many people who take a primitive view of the matter, what one might call a pre-legal view of the matter. They consider that MR. JAGGER has "got what was coming to him". They resent the anarchic quality of the Rolling Stones' performances, dislike their songs, dislike their influence on teenagers and broadly suspect them of decadence, a word used by MISS MONICA FURLONG in the *Daily Mail*.

As a sociological concern this may be reasonable enough, and at an emotional level it is very understandable, but it has nothing at all to do with the case. One has to ask a different question: has MR. JAGGER received the same treatment as he would have received if he had not been a famous figure, with all the criticism and resentment his celebrity has aroused? If a promising undergraduate had come back from a summer visit to Italy with four pep pills in his pocket would it have been thought right to ruin his career by sending him to prison for three months? Would it also have been thought necessary to display him handcuffed to the public?

There are cases in which a single figure becomes the focus for public concern about some aspect of public morality. The Stephen Ward case, with its dubious evidence and questionable verdict, was one of them, and that verdict killed STEPHEN WARD. There are elements of the same emotions in the reactions to this case. If we are going to make any case a symbol of the conflict between the sound traditional values of Britain and the new hedonism, then we must be sure that the sound traditional values include those of tolerance and equity. It should be the particular quality of British justice to ensure that MR. JAGGER is treated exactly the same as anyone else, no better and

Five years since the start of Beatlemania—Paul McCartney talks to RAY CONNOLLY . . .

FOUR FACES OF THE POLISHED BEATLE: FROM THE LEFT—AT BRIAN EPSTEIN'S MEMORIAL SERVICE • WITH ACTRESS JANE ASHER • EATING FISH AND CHIPS • AT HOME IN ST. JOHN'S WOOD

When you're a Beatle and you've got all the things money can buy . . .

PAUL McCARTNEY is beginning to look very much like his father. His cheeks have thinned and his nose is sharper and almost lop-sided. He's much less the baby-face.

When I visited him a couple of days before he went to India it was lunch time (mine) and breakfast time (his), and we had tea and toast, or what toast his pregnant Old English Sheepdog Martha hadn't tried to make off with.

His chin and neck were blue and rough, and his open pink shirt showed the freckles on his chest. He looked pale.

He's the only Beatle who lives in London. He had to, he says. He's the social Beatle. The one who never misses the best films or theatre, who turns up at the most first nights, who goes to the most fashionable clubs, who gets the most invitations to parties, and who accepts the most.

HE lives in St. John's Wood, behind a 10ft. high wall, and gates controlled by an electronic impulse from the house. There's a gas lamp with an electric bulb in the front garden.

"Living here is a necessity, because it's handy but quiet," says Paul McCartney.

PICTURES OF THE FAMILY

SINGING TO GET RICH

LISTEN TO OUR NEW DISC

DISCS

Part of the vast crowd of pop fans—estimated by the organisers at 500,000—listening to Mick Jagger (left) singing at a free lunch-time concert in Hyde Park, London, yesterday.

New clinic will cut motorway abortion trips

by CHRISTINE DOYLE, our Medical Reporter

Partnership

Requiem for a Stone

by JOHN GALE

BEFORE the Rolling Stones played in Hyde Park yesterday, Mick Jagger paid a tribute to the group's former guitarist, Brian Jones, who died in the swimming pool of his home last week.

Weedkiller brings canals back to life

A NEWLY DEVELOPED chemical has proved so successful in clearing weeds from a 25-mile stretch of the Chesterfield Canal, in Derbyshire, that the British Waterways Board may use it to reopen other canals that have fallen into disuse.

The chemical, Aquacide, eats away choking weeds without damaging other plants or animal life. Fish, insects and the plants on which they feed are unharmed. "Far from harming fish life," said a Waterways Board spokesman, "it actually gives them more room to swim about."

Cousins cuts race grants

(Continued from page 1)

Racked by disputes

MP moves to abolish law on obscenity

by our Political Staff

MR WILLIAM HAMLING is hoping to persuade a well-placed winner of the Private Members' ballot to sponsor the Bill to abolish the present restrictions on obscene publications which he introduced under the Ten-Minute Rule on 13 March.

INDEX

Milton Keynes UK
Ingram Content Group UK Ltd.
UKHW020010100923
428402UK00004B/13

9 781803 814933